A TASTE
OF EID

A TASTE OF EID

A CELEBRATION OF FOOD AND CULTURE
— RECIPES FOR EVERY OCCASION

BrunchBooks

هيئة الشارقة للكتاب
Sharjah Book Authority

10 9 8 7 6 5 4 3 2 1

Published in 2020 by Brunch Books, 14 Moulins Road, London E9 7EL
www.brunchbooks.co.uk

Text © Sharjah Book Authority 2020
Photography © Sharjah Book Authority 2020
Design © Sharjah Book Authority 2020

Book based on an original idea by Jacks Thomas
Recipe editor: Emma Marsden
Design and art direction: Kevan Westbury
Editor: Muna Reyal
Sharjah project management: Khoula Al Mujaini and Tasniem Roshdy
UK project management: Fiona Marsh
Food photography: Stuart Ovenden
Lifestyle photography: Barry Morgan
Food styling: Lisa Harrison, Anna Burges-Lumsden, Isla Murray
Assistant food styling: Sophie Gosling, Evie Harbury
Prop styling: Jenny Iggleden
Book production: David Brimble

This edition first published by Brunch Books in 2020

A CIP catalogue record for this book is available from the British Library

ISBN 978-1-9163291-0-2

Colour reproduction by Red Reprographics Ltd, London
Printed and bound in the UK by the Pureprint Group Ltd

**The oven temperatures given in the recipes are for a fan oven. If you are using a
conventional oven, please increase the temperature by 20°.**

CONTENTS

FOREWORD BY SALIHA MAHMOOD AHMED

As a child, Eid for me meant having pure, unadulterated fun, as other festivals did to my friends of all faiths. Twice a year, I remember playing games with my cousins, the smiling faces of elders, the smell of henna-laden hands, the jangle of gold bangles on my mother's arms, a myriad of colours and the smell of delicious food.

These memories remain very much alive in my memory and I feel that they provide a deep sense of comfort and security in this ever-changing world. Living in the UK, many people ask me what the festival of Eid means to me as a Muslim. For me, the answer is multi-layered because, as is true of all traditions, the significance of Eid changes and as I get older, there is a deeper spiritual value to the festivities.

With the passage of time, I came to realise that the two Eid festivals are quite distinct. While Eid-ul-Fitr follows a month of fasting called Ramadan – the ninth month of the Islamic lunar calendar – Eid-ul-Adha falls just after the annual pilgrimage of Hajj – at the end of the twelfth month of the lunar calendar. The spirit of each Eid festival differs.

Eid-ul-Adha commemorates the sacrifice made by Prophet Ibrahim for the sake of God, Allah. This is what gives this particular Eid the title of 'Feast of Sacrifice'. Eid-ul-Adha asks you to think about the transient nature of life and the importance of giving one's time and energy to help others and the pursuit of a spiritual nature. On the other hand, Eid-ul-Fitr comes as a gift for those who have been fasting for the month of Ramadan. Those who are able to fast will abstain from both eating and drinking anything, including water, between the hours of sunrise and sunset. Eid-ul-Fitr marks the end of Ramadan with spiritual reflection, prayers and a special meal. It's a period of celebration, hospitality and generosity, with time spent with friends and family.

These two Eid festivals and, of course, the month of Ramadan are arguably the most 'foodie' periods of the Islamic calendar. Culinary traditions span enormous geographical terrain, from Senegal to Indonesia, spreading wings through the Arab world, to lands touched by the great Mughal Emperors, the sophisticated cuisine of Persia and the heady scents and vigour of North African food. Fragrance, a soulful understanding of spice and a love for fresh herbs and locally sourced ingredients are the building blocks of our cuisine. Each part of the animal is used and respect for the environment and quality of produce is inherent in our cooking.

Thus, each recipe is never a mechanistic list of ingredients and instructions. Rather it is a gem of gastronomic knowledge tenderly passed down the generations, cooked with meticulous care and with the intention and profound fondness to feed family and friends. Food evolves gently with new culinary trends and the spread of the Muslim diaspora while at the same time holding fervently onto the practices and traditions of the past.

Through the recipes and anecdotes in this cookbook, you will be able to experience Eid from the table of a Muslim family, and not just one particular family, but a myriad of different families with differing cuisines. I hope that you will read these generous, celebratory recipes and savour the magical and almost spiritual quality of the food with your loved ones, sharing the universal message of Eid when you eat some of the most wonderful meals of your life together.

Saliha

Winner of Masterchef and author of
Khazana: A treasure trove of modern Mughal dishes

BREAKING THE FAST

Iftar, when the fast is broken, is a special moment during the month of Ramadan. Each culture and family does it slightly differently but many will eat a date to break the fast, along with a glass of water. This goes back to the days of the Prophet, whom it is said broke his fasts with three dates and a glass of water. Of course not everyone likes to eat dates or has access to them, so water alone works just as well too, but this ritual is often part of a quiet moment of reflection on the completion of another fast.

'When Eid al-Fitr comes, it brings happiness to everyone because it's time to end the fasting and return to a normal lifestyle.'

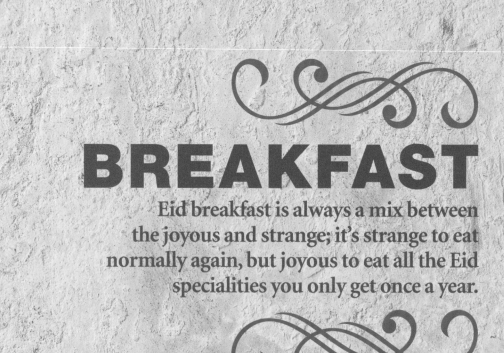

BREAKFAST

Eid breakfast is always a mix between the joyous and strange; it's strange to eat normally again, but joyous to eat all the Eid specialities you only get once a year.

EASY HOMEMADE GRANOLA

This is very easy to make – all the ingredients are mixed together first, then baked in the oven until crunchy. It stores well, too: cool in the tray first then pour into an airtight container and eat within two weeks – if it lasts that long…! Serve with creamy yogurt and fresh fruit.

Makes around 20 portions

For the dry mix
270g/2⅔ cups rolled oats
35g/¼ cup melon or
   pumpkin seeds
35g/¼ cup sesame seeds
2 tbsp flaxseeds
35g/⅓ cup unsweetened
   desiccated coconut
150g/1⅓ cup mixed nuts (use
   any combination of nuts)

For the wet ingredients
85g/¼ cup honey (you can
   also use maple or date syrup.
   Add more if you prefer your
   granola sweeter)
3 tbsp melted coconut oil
½ tsp cinnamon
2 tsp vanilla extract
a pinch of salt

Optional extras
150g/1 cup dried fruit (use any
   combination)

Preheat the oven to 180°C fan/400°F/gas mark 6 and line a large baking tray with baking parchment.

Tip the dry ingredients into a large bowl and mix together well. Then put all the wet ingredients into a small bowl and add 120ml/½ cup water. Whisk together, then pour onto the dry ingredients and fold everything together.

Tip the mixture onto the tray and spread evenly in a thin layer (this is important if you want a crunchy result). Bake for about 25 minutes, stirring and rotating midway (keep a close eye on the granola once the edges start to brown).

Remove from the oven, allow to cool completely and mix in the dried fruit. Store in an airtight container.

'As a child, I remember coming down the stairs in the morning to a waft of freshly cooked food and the table brimming with different curries and sweet foods.'

KHAMEER BREAD

These soft round buns can be turned into a sweet or savoury feast, depending on what you sprinkle over or fill them with. For a savoury bread, dust generously with za'atar or scatter over sesame seeds for a sweet flavour.

Makes 8

200ml/scant 1 cup warm water
7g/¼oz sachet dried active
  (not instant) yeast
1 tbsp sugar
pinch of saffron strands,
  lightly ground
300g/2⅔ cups plain flour,
  plus extra for dusting
1 tbsp milk powder
1 tsp salt
½ tsp ground cardamom,
  optional
1 medium egg, beaten

To sprinkle
½ tsp za'atar, for the
  savoury version
1 tbsp sesame seeds, for the
  sweet version

To serve
falafel and salad, for the
  savoury version:
date syrup, chopped dates,
  cream cheese, cinnamon, for
  the sweet version

Pour 50ml/¼ cup of the warm water into a small bowl and stir in the yeast and sugar. Set aside for 10 minutes until the yeast has dissolved and become frothy.

Measure the remaining 150ml/¾ cup of warm water into a jug and stir in the saffron. Allow to infuse and colour the water golden yellow; this will help to give the breads their distinctive colour.

Mix the flour, milk powder and salt in a large bowl. Add the cardamom if using. Gradually stir in the yeasted water and enough of the saffron water to give a soft, sticky dough. Mix well to bring together, it's not necessary to knead at this stage. The stickier and more elastic the dough, the better, as this will help it to puff up, so don't be tempted to add any extra flour. Cover the bowl loosely with a clean tea towel. Leave in a warm place to develop and rise for about 1 hour.

When the dough has risen and almost doubled in size, preheat the oven to its highest possible setting – 230°C fan/500°F/gas mark 9. Put one large or two smaller baking sheets towards the top of the oven to heat up.

On a lightly floured work surface, knock back the dough and knead briefly until smooth, then divide the dough into 8 equally-sized pieces. Dust your hands lightly with flour and form each piece into a ball, then flatten and roll or stretch to a disc of about 10cm/4in in diameter. Place on a tray lined with baking paper. The dough will be sticky and stretchy, don't worry if they are not perfect circles.

Brush with the beaten egg and sprinkle half of the discs with za'atar for the savoury version and the remainder with sesame seeds for the sweet version.

Quickly transfer the paper with the dough onto the baking sheet(s) in the oven. Bake near the top of the oven for 6–8 minutes, until golden and puffed up.

Either eat warm straight from the oven, or transfer to a cooling rack and allow to cool. Split open and fill with falafel and salad or a sweet mixture of date syrup, cream cheese and cinnamon.

ANDA GHOTALA

Here's our take on simple scrambled eggs. Finely chopped red onion cooked until just tender is livened up with lots of spices. The eggs are also hard-boiled, grated and cooked with a fragrant base of spiced onion mix. Serve with bread to mop it all up.

Serves 4

8 large eggs
2 tbsp unsalted butter or ghee
1 medium red onion
   (175–200g), finely chopped
1½ tbsp grated ginger
1½ tbsp finely chopped garlic
1 plump green chilli, seeds
   removed if preferred,
   finely chopped
3 medium tomatoes, chopped
rounded ¼ tsp turmeric
1½ tsp ground cumin
1½ tsp ground coriander
¾ tsp garam masala
salt and black pepper
4 tbsp fresh chopped coriander,
   plus extra to garnish
2–3 tbsp vegetable oil, for frying
pinch of chilli powder

Bring a large pan of water to the boil and lower 4 eggs into the water. Cook for 10 minutes until they are hard-boiled. Transfer the eggs to a bowl of cold water to cool. Once cool, peel and then coarsely grate into a bowl and set aside.

In a large frying pan or sauté pan, heat the butter or ghee, add the onion and fry on a medium–high heat for 4–5 minutes until the onion starts to soften. Lower the heat to medium. Add the ginger, garlic, chilli, tomatoes, spices and some salt and pepper. Stir-fry for 4–5 minutes until the tomatoes are very soft. Stir in the chopped fresh coriander. Pour in about 75ml /⅓ cup of water to give the mixture the consistency of a thick sauce, then mash with a potato masher to make a soft paste. Keep warm on a very low heat.

Heat the vegetable oil in a medium frying pan. Break the remaining 4 eggs into the pan (do this in 2 batches if necessary). Season with a pinch of salt, pepper and chilli powder and fry for 3–4 minutes, basting occasionally with the hot oil. Remove from the heat.

Meanwhile, stir the grated eggs into the spiced onion mixture. Simmer briefly, adding more water (about 75–100ml/⅓–scant ½ cup, as needed to make a consistency like soft scrambled eggs). Spoon into bowls and top each serving with a fried egg. Serve garnished with a scattering of fresh coriander.

YOGURT WITH SWEET-AND-SOUR CHICKPEAS

This refreshing breakfast combines creamy yogurt, finely grated cucumber and pops of pomegranate seeds, topped with a tangy combination of chickpeas and tamarind. Dress it up with mint leaves and serve with warm flatbreads. To prepare ahead, make the yogurt and the chickpeas separately and store in the fridge for up to two days.

Serves 4

450g/2 cups Greek yogurt
¼ cucumber, deseeded and
   finely grated
seeds from ½ pomegranate
a few mint leaves

**For the sweet-and-sour
chickpeas**
2 tbsp olive oil
1 small red onion, finely
   chopped
½ tsp ground coriander
400g/14oz can chickpeas,
   drained and liquid reserved
2 tbsp tamarind paste
½ lemon
salt and freshly ground
   black pepper

Spoon the yogurt into a bowl and stir in the grated cucumber and any juice. Season well. Set aside.

Next, make the sweet-and-sour chickpeas. Heat the oil in a medium frying pan over a medium heat and stir in the red onion. Stir-fry until the onion is golden and starting to soften – about 3–4 minutes.

Stir in the coriander, season well and cook for around 1 minute. Add a couple of tablespoons of the chickpea water and continue to cook until the liquid reduces and cooks into the onion and spice mixture. Stir in the tamarind paste and add a couple more tablespoons of chickpea liquid to combine everything together.

Tip the drained chickpeas into the pan and simmer for around 5 minutes until everything is heated through and the sauce reduces slightly. Season with a squeeze of lemon juice and salt and pepper. Set aside.

Stir about half the pomegranate seeds carefully into the yogurt and spoon into four bowls.

Spoon the chickpeas evenly among the bowls, then top with the rest of the pomegranate and garnish with a few mint leaves.

BALALEET

Here's one of our classic breakfast dishes – fine strands of vermicelli, cooked in a sugar syrup and flavoured with cinnamon in a cardomom-scented omelette. The sweet pasta is then topped with a large omelette which is subtly flavoured with cardamom. It's delicious and served on one large platter for everyone to tuck in.

Serves 4–6

1 tbsp rosewater
a good pinch of saffron strands
100g/½ cup sugar
1 cinnamon stick
4 cardamom pods
1 tbsp sunflower oil
230g/8oz fine vermicelli
25g /¼ stick butter
½ tsp ground cinnamon, optional
4 large eggs
a pinch of salt
¼ tsp ground cardamom (or grind the seeds from around 10 cardamom pods)
sunflower oil, ghee or butter, to fry

Mix the rosewater and saffron strands in a small bowl and set aside.

Pour in the sugar into a pan, then add the cinnamon, cardamom and 400ml/1⅔ cups of water. Bring to the boil over a medium–high heat and cook until the sugar has dissolved and a light syrup forms. This will take around 5–10 minutes. Set aside.

In a large pan, heat the oil over a medium–high heat and boil a full kettle.

Add the vermicelli to the pan and fry for a couple of minutes until it turns a light golden colour. Add enough boiling water to just cover and simmer the vermicelli for 2–3 minutes. Drain. Add the butter and melt, add the cooked vermicelli and stir it into the butter to coat. Add the ground cinnamon, if using. This will give the vermicelli a darker hue and the distinctive cinnamon flavour.

Remove the cinnamon stick and cardamom pods from the pan of sugar and pour a third of the syrup over the vermicelli. Simmer for another couple of minutes until the liquid is absorbed. Gradually add more syrup if required until the vermicelli is nicely coated in the syrup but not drowning in it – you might not need all the syrup and any leftover syrup can be kept for 2–3 days. Stir in the rosewater and saffron. Remove the pan from the heat and tip onto a serving plate. Cover to keep warm while you make the omelette.

To make the omelette, crack the eggs into a mixing bowl, season with salt, add the ground cardamom and whisk together.

Heat a large frying pan over a medium heat and add a drizzle of oil or knob of butter or ghee. When the oil has heated through or the ghee or butter melted, pour in the eggs and swirl them around the pan. Leave to cook for about a minute to set most of the mixture, then start to draw in the edges with a spatula, tipping the pan slightly to allow the egg to run into the holes and more egg to set. When the omelette is just set, fold over and slide out of the pan on top of the Balaleet. Serve immediately.

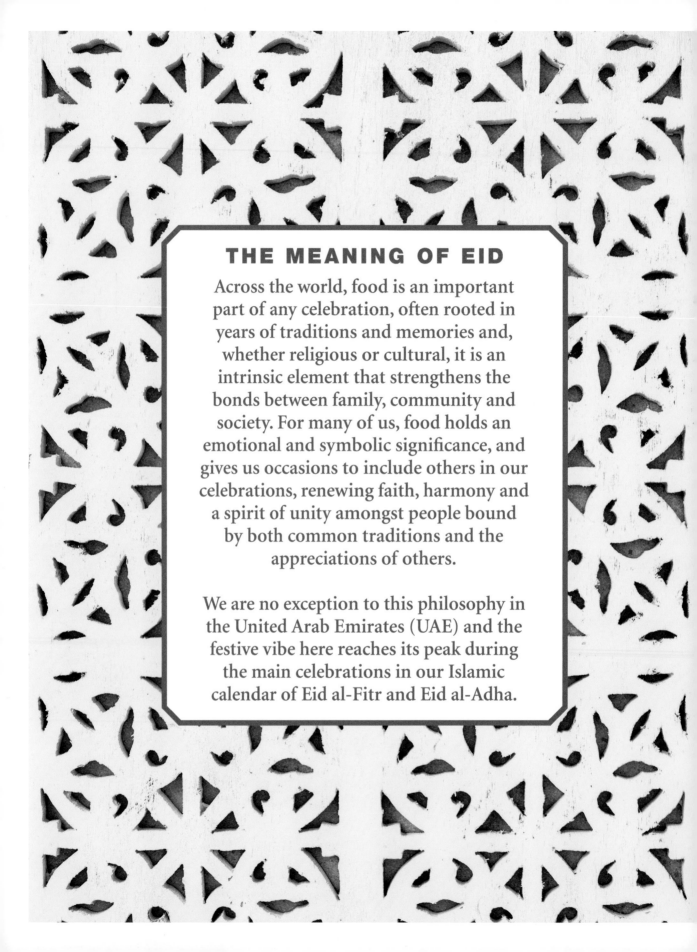

THE MEANING OF EID

Across the world, food is an important part of any celebration, often rooted in years of traditions and memories and, whether religious or cultural, it is an intrinsic element that strengthens the bonds between family, community and society. For many of us, food holds an emotional and symbolic significance, and gives us occasions to include others in our celebrations, renewing faith, harmony and a spirit of unity amongst people bound by both common traditions and the appreciations of others.

We are no exception to this philosophy in the United Arab Emirates (UAE) and the festive vibe here reaches its peak during the main celebrations in our Islamic calendar of Eid al-Fitr and Eid al-Adha.

ROTI WITH PANEER AND SPINACH

Sweet red onion, spinach and paneer turn these simple flatbreads into a special breakfast with a spiced filling seasoned with ground cardamom, a touch of zesty lime powder and curry powder. Try serving this with a dollop of thick creamy yogurt or a fried egg.

Makes 8

For the roti
150g/scant 1½ cups wholemeal flour
100g/scant 1 cup plain flour, plus extra for dusting
1 tsp salt
1 tbsp vegetable oil, plus extra for frying

For the filling
1 tbsp vegetable oil
1 small red onion, finely sliced
2 tsp grated fresh ginger
½ tsp dehn khaneen spice mix, (see below)
75g/⅓ cup spinach, washed and well drained
75g/⅓ cup paneer, grated or finely crumbled
Salt and pepper, to taste

Dehn khaneen spice mix
½ tsp ground cardamom
pinch dried lime powder
1 tsp mild curry powder
1 tsp turmeric
½ tsp ground cloves
½ tsp ground black pepper

Put both types of flour into a large bowl and stir in the salt. Add the oil and gradually add 150ml/⅔ cup of water to make a soft dough.

Knead for a few minutes until smooth, then cover and leave to rest for a minimum of 30 minutes.

Meanwhile, make the filling. Heat the oil in a frying pan over a medium heat. Fry the onion for 5–6 minutes, stirring occasionally, until softened.

Mix together the dehn khaneen spices and stir into the pan with the ginger. Continue to fry for 2–3 minutes.

Add the spinach in handfuls, stirring continually until it wilts. This will take 3–4 minutes – you want to keep the mixture as dry as possible, so don't be tempted to add any extra liquid.

Stir in the paneer and season to taste. Set aside and allow to cool.

When you're ready to make the roti, divide the dough into 8 pieces. Lightly dust the worktop and roll each piece into a circle of about 12cm/4¾in in diameter.

Spoon 1–2 tablespoons of the filling mixture into the centre of each circle and pull up the edges, pinching them together to enclose the filling.

Roll the parcels as thinly as possible, to about 12–14cm/4¾–5½in in diameter, ensuring that the filling doesn't break through the dough.

Heat a drizzle of oil in a frying pan over a medium–high heat. Cook one roti at a time for 2–3 minutes on each side until browned and slightly puffed.

Keep warm and repeat until all the roti are cooked. Serve immediately.

KHABEESA

This is crumbly and full of texture. It's made by cooking flour and mixing it with a golden-hued light sugar syrup that is infused with saffron and then mixed with spices and nuts. It's like a spiced crumble – and very tasty – and can be eaten at breakfast or dessert.

Serves 8–12

350g/3¼ cups plain flour
225g/1 cup caster sugar
1 pinch of saffron strands, lightly ground
a small pinch of salt
1 tsp ground cardamom
¼–½ tsp ground turmeric
1 tbsp rosewater
225g/scant 1 cup ghee
100g/scant 1 cup ground almonds
30g/scant ⅓ cup slivered pistachios (or chopped pistachios)
30g/scant ⅓ cup flaked almonds

Heat a large, heavy-based pan over a medium heat, add the flour and toast until it turns a light golden brown – this will take about 10 minutes. Watch and stir the flour continually to make sure it doesn't burn, otherwise it will taste bitter.

Meanwhile, pour 500ml/2¼ cups water into a medium pan and add the sugar. Add the saffron and slowly bring to the boil so that the colour and flavour of the saffron infuses the water.

When the flour is ready, stir in the salt, cardamom and turmeric then gradually pour the sugar syrup into the flour mixture, little by little, and mix well with a spatula. It will start to clump but keep going until all the liquid is combined. Stir in the rosewater to taste.

With the pan still over a low heat, add the ghee. Once it's melted and absorbed into the mixture, stir in the ground almonds, pistachios and flaked almonds. Stir together well until the mixture looks crumbly.

Spoon into a tray, then set aside to cool.

To serve, spoon into a serving dish and serve cold.

CHEBAB WITH DATE MOLASSES

These pancakes have a lovely texture – soft and slightly aerated. They're not too sweet, but the rosewater and cardamom give a distinctive taste while the saffron colours the pancakes a warm golden shade. A drizzle of date syrup provides a rich deep fruit flavour at the end.

Makes 12

500ml/2¼ cups lukewarm water
4 pinches of saffron strands
350g/3¼ cups plain flour
4 tbsp milk powder
½ tbsp baking powder
1½ tbsp dried yeast
   (not instant yeast)
2 tbsp caster sugar
1–2 tsp ground cardamom
1 large egg
2 tsp sunflower oil
1 tbsp rosewater
sunflower oil, for frying

To serve
date molasses (or syrup)

Pour the lukewarm water into a jug. Add the saffron and leave to soak so that the colour infuses the water.

Put the flour into a large bowl. Add the milk powder, baking powder, dried yeast, sugar and ground cardamom. Mix everything together. Make a well in the middle and whisk in the egg, then gradually add the saffron water to make a smooth batter. Stir in the oil and rosewater. Cover and leave in the fridge for at least 6 hours or overnight until it is full of bubbles and well aerated.

When you're ready to cook the pancakes, take the batter out of the fridge. Give it a good stir to knock back the air and make a smooth thick batter again.

Heat a non-stick 20cm/8in frying pan over a medium–high heat and add a drizzle of oil. When hot, pour a small ladleful of batter into the pan and swirl it round to cover the base. Cook for 1–2 minutes until bubbles appear and the top is set, then flip it over and cook the other side for another 1–2 minutes. Reduce the heat so that the pancakes don't burn.

Once cooked, transfer to a plate and keep warm. Repeat until you've used up all the batter to make 12 pancakes.

Put 2 folded pancakes per person on a plate and drizzle with the date molasses. Serve immediately.

CRISP FILO PARCELS WITH LEFTOVER LAMB

These little parcels made with filo pastry and garnished with a sprinkling of cumin seeds and lemon-scented sumac make the most of leftovers. They make a great brunch, served with ripe tomatoes, yogurt drizzled in tamarind or tahini and, of course, a pot of coffee on the side.

Makes 6 parcels

around 600g/4 cups leftover
  lamb, rice and vegetables
  from Lamb Ghouzi (page 98)
100g/⅔ cup frozen peas,
  thawed
30g/⅓ stick butter or ghee,
  melted and cooled
2–3 tbsp freshly chopped parsley
freshly ground black pepper
olive oil, for brushing
12 sheets filo pastry
  (220g/8oz packet)
sumac and cumin seeds

Preheat the oven to 180°C fan/400°F/gas mark 6. Lightly oil 2 baking sheets.

Extract the lamb and vegetables from the rice and chop it all up, then return it to the rice. Use a fork to mix everything together – this will help to separate the grains of rice, too. Add the peas, butter or ghee and parsley, season with black pepper and mix together.

Pour some olive oil into a small bowl. Take two of the filo pastry sheets and put one on top of the other on a board, with the longest edge horizontal. Cut them both in half vertically through the middle to make four long rectangles of filo.

Working with one of the rectangles, brush lightly with oil. Take another piece and brush that lightly with oil, then lay it on top of the first piece crossways. Do the same again with the other two pieces, this time putting them on top diagonally from top left to bottom right and the other piece from top right to bottom left. You'll have a rough star at the end.

Spoon around one sixth of the mixture into the middle. Lift up one of the corners of the layered pastry and put it on top of the mixture, give it a quick brush with the oil and continue to work all the way round to make a rough parcel. All the filling will be covered at this stage. Brush the top lightly with oil again and sprinkle some sumac and cumin seeds over the top. Lift onto the baking sheet.

Do the same again with the rest of the pastry and filling to make 5 more parcels, putting them onto the baking sheet as you go.

Bake in the oven for 25–30 minutes until golden and crisp. Turn the oven trays halfway through if they're browning more on one side.

Cool until warm and serve.

LUNCH

A time for sharing different foods among friends and family. An overflowing table, with many hands reaching for so many dishes.

DANGO

This classic chickpea recipe makes a perfect starter that is served in small bowls with a big wedge of lemon to squeeze over. The spicing is very subtle as the spices are added to the liquid that the chickpeas have been cooked in, to infuse with just a gentle hint of flavour.

Serves 6

500g/2½ cups dried
   chickpeas
2 dried lemons
2 dried red chillies
salt, to taste
½ tsp black pepper
½ tsp cumin powder, roasted

To serve
olive oil, to drizzle
1 lemon, cut into six wedges

The night before you want to make this, pick over the dried chickpeas and discard any bits of grit then put them in a large bowl. Pour in 2.5 litres/4 pints 8fl oz cold water and leave to soak overnight.

The next day, drain, then rinse under cold running water.

Tip the chickpeas into a large saucepan and add 5 litres/8 pints 16 fl oz water. Cover the pan and bring to the boil.

When the water starts to boil, lift off any scum that forms on top with a slotted spoon. Reduce the heat and continue to simmer the chickpeas for 40–50 minutes, until the chickpeas are soft.

Add the dried lemons and the dried red chillies and continue to simmer for around 10 minutes to infuse the flavour into the liquid.

Take the pan off the heat and season with salt, pepper and cumin. Spoon into bowls and serve hot with a drizzle of olive oil, a lemon wedge and an extra grinding of black pepper, if you like.

KOHLRABI AND CARROT SALAD

Kohlrabi is a green or purple bulbous vegetable with smooth skin and slight bumps where the roots grow. It has a simple flavour with the same crisp texture as carrots and comes to life with subtle spices and fresh herbs. This dish can be made and served straightaway, but it also stores well in the fridge for up to a day before serving.

Serves 6–8

500g/2 cups kohlrabi, peeled
300g /2 cups carrots, peeled
1 tsp cumin seeds
1½ tsp fennel seeds
2 tbsp olive oil
2 tbsp lemon juice
1 tbsp clear honey
15g/⅔ cup freshly chopped
    flat-leaf parsley
15g/⅔ cup freshly chopped
    mint
1 tsp black mustard seeds
salt and freshly ground
    black pepper

Shred the kohlrabi and carrots in a food processor or use a mandolin or coarse grater.

Put the cumin seeds and fennels seeds into a small pan and heat gently until aromatic and beginning to toast. Crush them lightly in a pestle and mortar or use the bottom of a mug on a chopping board.

In a small bowl, whisk together the oil, lemon juice and honey. Stir in the crushed seeds, parsley, mint, mustard seeds, and salt and pepper to taste.

Put the kohlrabi and carrot into a serving bowl. Pour over the dressing and toss well together.

BARLEY, POMEGRANATE AND CHAMEE SALAD

This salad is special because it involves preparing fresh cheese at home. Making chamee cheese isn't popular now, but it was made more when fewer types of cheese were available. It is actually the rich, creamy butter that is scooped out when heating labna. It looks and tastes very similar to cottage cheese, but is a little saltier.

Serves 4–6

For the salad
100g/½ cup pearl barley
50g/generous 2 cups rocket, roughly chopped
15g/⅔ cup parsley, roughly chopped
10g/⅓ cup mint leaves, leaves picked and roughly chopped
seeds from 1 large pomegranate
4 spring onions, finely chopped

For the chamee cheese
200g/scant 1 cup labna or full-fat cream cheese

For the dressing
3 tbsp olive oil
2 tbsp balsamic vinegar
1 tsp ground cumin
1 garlic clove, crushed
salt and black pepper to taste

Start by cooking the pearl barley. Put it into a medium pan and cover with plenty of cold water. Cover and bring to the boil. As soon as the water is boiling, skim off any scum and half cover the pan with the lid. Reduce the heat and simmer for 45 minutes until tender.

Next make the cheese. Scoop the labna or cream cheese into a frying pan and sprinkle with a little salt. Place the pan over a gentle heat and cook very slowly for 5–8 minutes until the liquid evaporates. It'll start to look crumbly and very like a dry cottage cheese. Turn the mixture every now and then.

When the barley is ready, drain well, put into a large bowl and allow to cool. Mix together all the ingredients for the dressing, seasoning to taste.

Add the rocket, parsley and mint to the bowl of pearl barley, followed by the pomegranate seeds and spring onion.

Pour over the dressing and toss well. Spoon the chamee on top, roughly mix in and serve.

MOUTABEL

This classic dip is made from roasting aubergines until tender and charred. The flesh is then mixed with tahini, garlic, chilli and cumin. For a creamier flavour or to serve a few more, stir in 3 tablespoons of plain yogurt after blending. Give the spices time to meld together by making this a day ahead and it will have a lovely mellow taste.

Serves 4

For the moutabel

2 aubergines, each about
   275g/10oz
2 tbsp tahini
1–2 garlic cloves, crushed
   or finely grated
½ plump, mild green chilli
   (1 tbsp chopped green chilli),
   seeds left in or removed
   according to taste
2 tbsp olive oil, plus extra
   for drizzling
2 tbsp lemon juice
¼ tsp ground cumin
½ tsp salt
flatbread, to serve

For the topping

½ small, trimmed cauliflower
   (about 340g/12oz), broken
   into florets and sliced
   1cm/½in thick
2 tbsp olive oil
¼ tsp ground cumin
¼ tsp salt
good pinch of paprika
handful of pine nuts, toasted
small handful of freshly
   chopped flat leaf parsley or
   coriander

Preheat the oven to 200°C fan/425°F/gas mark 7. Prick the aubergines all over with a fork a few times, then lay them on a baking sheet. Roast for 35–40 minutes or until they feel soft and tender and the skins are slightly charred.

After about 15 minutes of roasting time, make the topping. Line a baking tray with baking parchment and lay the cauliflower on it. Mix the oil, cumin, salt and paprika in a small bowl. Drizzle this over the cauliflower then gently toss together so the cauliflower is coated. Spread out in a single layer on the baking tray and roast for about 20 minutes, turning once, until slightly charred.

When the aubergines are softened, remove from the oven and when cool enough to handle, peel off the skins. Roughly chop the aubergine flesh and put it into a food processor with the tahini, garlic, chilli, oil, lemon juice, cumin and salt and blend together until smooth. Taste and adjust seasonings.

Serve the moutabel in one large or 4 small bowls, topped with a little of the roasted cauliflower, pine nuts, a scattering of parsley or coriander and a drizzle of olive oil.

Serve warm or cold with flatbread and the rest of the cauliflower, for dipping.

VEGETABLE AND OAT SOUP

This has a lovely silky creamy texture, thickened with oats. The soy and coriander give an Asian flavour while the fennel gives an aniseed note. It is best made and eaten on the same day because it thickens up overnight as the oats swell. If you do reheat the soup, add a little extra water or stock until it reaches the desired consistency.

Serves 6–8

2 tbsp olive oil

1 onion, finely diced

1 tsp fennel seeds, optional

1 garlic clove, diced

1 medium carrot, cut into
    small dice

1 medium-sized potato, peeled
    and cut into small dice

1 stick of celery, cut into
    small dice

198g/7oz can sweetcorn,
    drained

2 tbsp soy sauce

2 tbsp coriander leaves,
    roughly chopped

about 1.5 litres/2½ pints hot
    chicken or vegetable stock

125g/generous ⅔ cup porridge
    oats (not jumbo)

salt and freshly ground
    black pepper

juice of 1 lemon

2 tbsp freshly chopped parsley,
    to garnish

In a medium saucepan, heat the olive oil over a medium heat. Stir in the onion and the fennel seeds, if using, and cook for about 5 minutes, until the onion has started to soften.

Add the garlic, carrot, potato and celery. Season with black pepper. Continue to cook for about 5 minutes, stirring every now and then.

Add the sweetcorn, soy sauce, coriander leaves and hot stock and let simmer until the vegetables are almost soft, about 5 minutes.

Pour the oats into a bowl. Using a ladle, take some of the stock from the pan and pour into the bowl with the oats and stir well, adding more ladlefuls until the stock is absorbed and the oats start to thicken.

Pour the oats mixture back into the pan and continue to cook the soup for another 8–10 minutes, stirring from time to time until the oats are cooked through and the soup has thickened.

Taste and season with salt and more black pepper if desired. Lastly stir in the lemon juice.

Take the pan off the heat, ladle into bowls and garnish with the parsley.

THE MEANING OF EID

Perhaps the biggest and most known celebration in the Islamic calendar is Eid al-Fitr, the end of the holy month of Ramadan, a solemn period of contemplation and reflection during which Muslims throughout the world fast during daylight hours. After breaking our fast with dates and water, meals are taken together and you will find some of the recipes such as Arseeyah, a chicken and rice stew, and Khanfaroosh, mini saffron and cardamom cakes, in this book. Full of flavours and textures, Emirati cuisine is influenced by the ingredients found growing in its oases, desert and mountains; spices traded in its historic souks, seafood fished along its coast and dates plucked straight from palm trees. Connecting our food and traditions with non-Emiratis and non-Muslims is a simple pleasure that we, as hospitable people, greatly enjoy.

LENTIL SOUP

With just a few storecupboard ingredients, this soup is quick and simple to make. It's warm and comforting, with a gentle level of spices and can be livened up with a squeeze of lime at the end. You can make this soup one or two days ahead and it also freezes well for up to three months.

Serves 4

3 tbsp olive or vegetable oil, plus extra for drizzling
1 small and 1 medium onion
200g/scant 1 cup dried red lentils
1 medium carrot, diced
2 garlic cloves, crushed or finely grated
1 tsp ground cumin
½ tsp turmeric
1 tsp garam masala
¼ tsp ground cardamom (or crushed seeds)
½ tsp salt
1.25 litres/5½ cups hot vegetable or chicken stock
ground black pepper
lime wedges, optional

Pour 1 tablespoon of the oil into a small saucepan. Halve the small onion lengthways and finely slice. Heat the oil in the pan and when hot, add the onion and a pinch of salt and fry on a medium heat for about 15 minutes or until golden. Stir occasionally so the onion browns evenly and becomes crispy, adjusting the heat as necessary. Remove with a slotted spoon and drain, spread out on a plate lined with kitchen paper. Set aside.

Rinse the lentils in a sieve. Chop the remaining onion. Pour the remaining 2 tablespoons of oil into a large saucepan and heat. Add the onion and carrot and fry for 6–7 minutes, or until the onion has softened, stirring occasionally.

Add the garlic and cook, stirring, for 1 minute. Mix in the cumin, turmeric, garam masala, cardamom and salt and stir for 1 minute, then add the lentils and stock. Bring to a boil, then lower the heat and simmer, covered, for about 20 minutes, until the lentils are completely cooked. Season to taste with pepper.

Blend the soup until smooth. Serve in bowls scattered with the crispy onions and a drizzle of olive oil. If you like a touch of sharpness, serve with lime wedges on the side for squeezing into the soup.

SEAFOOD SOUP

This recipe calls for whole prawns so that once peeled, the shells are used to infuse the finished stock. A dried lime is essential here – it is used at the beginning in the stock then cooked further with the other ingredients to produce a wonderfully musky citrus flavour. Give it a good squeeze to extract all the juices at the end.

Serves 4

600g/1¼lb prawns, shell on
2 bay leaves
1 dried lime, pierced 3–4 times
6 black peppercorns
2 tbsp olive oil
1 onion, roughly chopped
1 fat garlic clove, sliced
1 tbsp tomato purée
1 tsp ground coriander
a pinch of chilli powder
¼ tsp ground turmeric
¼ tsp ground cumin
500g/3 cups potatoes, peeled
    and chopped
1 red pepper, diced
2 tbsp freshly chopped
    flat-leaf parsley
salt and freshly ground
    black pepper

To serve
1 lime, quartered

Peel the prawns, then put all the heads and shells in a large saucepan. Pour in 1.2 litres/5⅓ cups of cold water and add the bay leaves, dried lime and the peppercorns. Cover and bring to the boil. As soon as the water is boiling, reduce the heat to a simmer and cook for 15 minutes. Strain the liquid through a sieve and into a bowl. Reserve the dried lime.

While the stock is cooking, devein and butterfly the prawns: take a sharp knife and run it down the back of the prawns to open up the skin at the back and release the vein (discard this). Take the knife slightly deeper into the back so that when the prawn cooks it will open slightly like a butterfly. Do the same with all the prawns.

Return the (empty) pan to the hob and add the olive oil and onion and cook over a medium heat for around 5 minutes until the onion is starting to turn golden. Stir in the garlic and cook for 1 minute, then stir in the tomato purée, coriander, chilli powder, turmeric and cumin and season well. Stir in 1–2 tablespoons of the stock and cook for a further 1–2 minutes to cook the spices.

Stir in the reserved dried lime, the potatoes and red pepper, then pour over the stock. Cover and simmer for 10 minutes until the potatoes are tender. Add the prawns and simmer for 3 minutes or until all the prawns have turned pink. Squeeze the juice out of the dried lime and into the soup, then discard. Stir in half the parsley.

Ladle among four bowls and serve with the remaining parsley sprinkled over the top and a wedge of lime for each person to squeeze over.

HATTA ROLL WITH CAMEL SOUR CREAM SAUCE

This dish is new in Emirati cuisine. Hatta roll, combining flatbread with spiced chicken, salad and homemade soured cream, is a fusion of the culture and traditional flavours of Eid and Emirati cuisine. This is shown through the camel cream and local spices, which give it the traditional Emirati taste.

Serves 4

100g/generous ½ cup camel
  cream or double cream
1½ tsp lemon juice
600g/1¼lb skinless and
  boneless chicken thighs
¾ tsp ground paprika
1 slightly heaped tsp Arabic
  spices – use a mix of ground
  cardamom, turmeric, black
  pepper and ground coriander
a little olive oil, for drizzling
4 flatbreads or wraps
2 tbsp harissa paste
4 large lettuce leaves
30g/⅓ cup white onion,
  thinly sliced
60g/⅓ cup tomatoes,
  thinly sliced
salt and freshly ground
  black pepper

Put the camel or double cream into a small bowl. Rest the bowl over a larger bowl filled with ice cubes and whisk until slightly thickened. Stir in the lemon juice and season with salt and pepper. Transfer the bowl to the fridge to keep chilled.

Preheat the grill. Line a board with clingfilm and lay the chicken thighs on top. Cover with another piece of clingfilm. Flatten with a rolling pin until they are around 1cm/½in thick and double their original size. Season with the paprika, Arabic spices and salt and pepper. Rub a little oil over each piece.

Lay on a lipped baking sheet and grill for 5–7 minutes on each side until cooked. Check they're cooked all the way through by piercing the thickest part to see the juices run clear. If they're still pink, continue to grill until clear and the chicken is cooked through.

Lay the flatbread out on four plates and spread each with ½ tbsp harissa. Next divide the lettuce, chicken, onion and tomato evenly between each wrap. Roll up with one end closed and toast in a panini maker. Slice diagonally and serve with the camel sour cream and extra salad.

See recipe overleaf

SEHNAH TACOS

This is an Emirati-Mexican twist on a classic taco with its side dishes. Every component represents an element in the traditional meal that people along the Gulf had in the form of mini tacos. Remember that the tortillas firm up as soon as they start to cool, so make these last so that they're still warm and flexible as you fill them.

Makes 6 tacos

For the red cabbage pickle
½ small red cabbage, core removed
250ml/generous 1 cup clear malt vinegar or apple cider vinegar
1 tsp sea salt
additional flavourings: celery seeds, onion powder, garlic powder, peppercorn

Use a mandolin or the slicer attachment on a food processor to slice the cabbage finely.

Pour the vinegar into a medium saucepan and add 250ml/generous 1 cup water and the salt. Heat to dissolve the salt, then add the cabbage. Add any of the additional flavourings you fancy. Increase the heat and bring to the boil.

Cover the pan and reduce the heat to medium. Cook for 20–30 minutes, stirring occasionally.

Take the pan off the heat and set aside to cool.

Spoon into a food processor and whizz to finely chop the pieces. Any leftover cabbage can be stored in an airtight container. Eat within a week.

For the Khaneen Avocado Smash
2 ripe avocados
juice of 2 limes
1–2 tsp dehn khaneen (see cook's tip, below)
1 tsp cumin seeds
salt and freshly ground black pepper

Halve the avocados and carefully remove the stone. Scoop the flesh out with a spoon and put into a small bowl.

Add the remaining ingredients and use a fork to roughly mash everything together. Season to taste, cover and set aside.

> *Cook's tip*
> *To make the dehn khaneen spice mix, put ½ tsp ground cardamom in a bowl. Add a pinch of dried lime powder, 1 tsp mild curry powder, 1 tsp turmeric, ½ tsp ground cloves and ½ tsp ground black pepper. Spoon into a jar and store in a dark place.*

For the Pico de Gallo (salsa salad)
1 medium red onion, diced
1 medium tomato, diced
1 tbsp fresh dill, finely chopped
juice of 1 lime
¼–½ tsp dry lime powder

Put all the ingredients into a bowl, season to taste, cover and set aside.

For the tortillas
70g/⅔ cup maize flour or fine ground cornmeal or fine polenta
70g/⅔ cup plain flour, plus extra for dusting
½ tsp baking powder
a pinch of fine salt
2 tbsp vegetable oil
4 tbsp hot water

Put the maize, cornmeal or polenta into a medium bowl. Add the flour and baking powder and season with the salt.

Make a well in the middle and pour in the oil, followed by the hot water. Mix everything together to make a dough, then transfer to a clean, lightly floured surface and knead until smooth.

Divide the dough into 6 even-sized pieces. Roll each into a ball and cover with clingfilm. Set aside for 10 minutes to rest.

Lightly flour a board and roll each ball into rounds, approximately 12cm/5in in diameter, keeping the shape as even as possible.

Heat a flat, heavy-based frying pan over a medium-high heat (no oil required) and cook each tortilla for about 1 minute, until lightly risen and slightly brown, on each side. The time will vary depending on how hot the pan is. Set aside on a plate as soon as you cook each one.

To serve
6–12 marinated anchovies
radish, sliced
rocket

To assemble, place the tortillas on a board or plate and start with a spoonful of the avocado smash. Spread it out and top it with the pico de gallo, a spoonful of the chopped red cabbage pickle, the anchovies, some radish and some rocket leaves.

MIXED VEGETABLE KURMA

All the ingredients in this curry are easy to get hold of and combine to give a wonderfully spiced aromatic flavour to the vegetables. The addition of yogurt and milk combine to give the kurma its intrinsic creamy taste – make sure you use full-fat as it can be heated without curdling. Serve with basmati rice for a satisfying lunch.

Serves 4

2 tbsp vegetable oil

1 tbsp ghee

2 medium onions, diced

3 garlic cloves, finely chopped

2.5cm/1in piece root ginger, peeled and roughly chopped

25g/¼ cup raw cashew nuts, chopped

1 cinnamon stick, in half

1 plump, mild green chilli, deseeded (optional) and finely chopped

1 tsp garam masala

1 tsp ground cumin

½ tsp ground coriander

½ tsp ground turmeric

½ tsp ground cardamom

¼ tsp ground fennel seeds

¾ tsp salt, or to taste

2 medium tomatoes, chopped

100ml (scant ½ cup) full-fat milk

2 medium carrots

115g/¾ cup fine green beans,

100g/⅔ cup frozen peas

125g (generous ½ cup) natural full-fat yogurt

freshly ground black pepper

handful fresh coriander, chopped

basmati rice, to serve

Heat the oil and ghee in a large saucepan. Add the onion and fry on a medium heat for about 15 minutes until softened and starting to turn brown, stirring occasionally. Remove the pan from the heat. Put about a third of the onions into a mini blender, or the small bowl of a food processor, with the garlic, ginger, nuts and 2 tablespoons water and process to make a thickish paste. Set aside.

Put the pan with the onion back on the heat. Stir the cinnamon pieces, green chilli, ½ tsp of the garam masala and the rest of the ground spices and the salt into the onion and stir fry for 2 minutes. Add the tomatoes and garlic and ginger paste into the pan and stir fry until the tomatoes have softened and broken down, about 5 minutes.

Stir in 200ml/scant 1 cup water and the milk. Chop the carrots and trim and slice the green beans. Add the carrots and simmer, covered, for 12–15 minutes, until they are just starting to soften. Stir in the beans and cook for about 15 minutes or until the carrots and beans are tender but still hold their shape. Add the peas and simmer for 2 minutes. Remove and discard the cinnamon pieces.

Stir in the yogurt, the remaining ½ tsp garam masala and a grinding of black pepper. Simmer gently for 2 minutes. If you want to thin the kurma sauce, add a splash more water.

Garnish with fresh coriander and serve with basmati rice.

'Eid is a time for family, no matter how big or small, and sharing food among all of us. Of course, there's always lots of good banter over which is our favourite dish!'

CHICKEN AND CHICKPEA CURRY

This crowd-pleasing stew has simple, spiced flavours with a subtle kick of heat from the chilli powder. If you prefer it a bit spicier, sprinkle in a pinch or two more or use a medium or hot chilli powder.

Serves 4

4 tbsp olive oil
1 large onion, diced
1 tsp ground cumin
4 garlic cloves, finely chopped
1 tsp mild chilli powder
1 tsp turmeric
1 tsp salt
1 x 227g/8oz can chopped
    tomatoes
2 large skinless, boneless
    chicken breasts, cubed
400g/14oz can chickpeas,
    drained
1 tsp garam masala
2 tbsp full-fat Greek yogurt
handful of fresh coriander,
    leaves and sprigs, chopped

To serve
steamed basmati rice and/or
    flat bread

Heat the olive oil in a large saucepan, and then stir in the onion and cumin. Fry on a medium heat for about 12–15 minutes until golden brown, stirring occasionally and adjusting the heat as needed.

Add the garlic, chilli powder, turmeric, salt and tomatoes and cook over a medium heat for 4–5 minutes, until the mixture starts to stick to the bottom of the pan. Stir in 125ml/½ cup water and cover the pan with a lid. Turn the heat down to the lowest setting and leave to cook for 5 minutes until the oil separates from the sauce.

Remove the lid, stir in the chicken and fry on a medium–high heat for 5–8 minutes until the chicken is cooked through, stirring occasionally. Tip in the chickpeas and 250ml/generous 1 cup water and bring to a simmer. Put the lid back on the pan and cook on a low heat for a further 7 minutes. Remove the lid and continue to simmer for about 7 minutes more, or until about half of the liquid has evaporated and the sauce has thickened.

Over a medium heat, stir in the garam masala and yogurt and simmer for 3 minutes.

Remove from the heat and garnish with fresh coriander. Serve hot with steamed basmati rice and/or flat bread.

Cook's tip
If you want to prepare this ahead, spoon into a sealable container and cool after simmering the garam masala and yogurt. Seal and chill for up to three days. It can also be frozen for up to a month. Thaw at a cool room temperature and reheat until completely heated through. Garnish with coriander to serve.

'The best Eid feeling is when families get together and enjoy the finest home-cooked food, prepared by our own Michelin chefs — our mothers!'

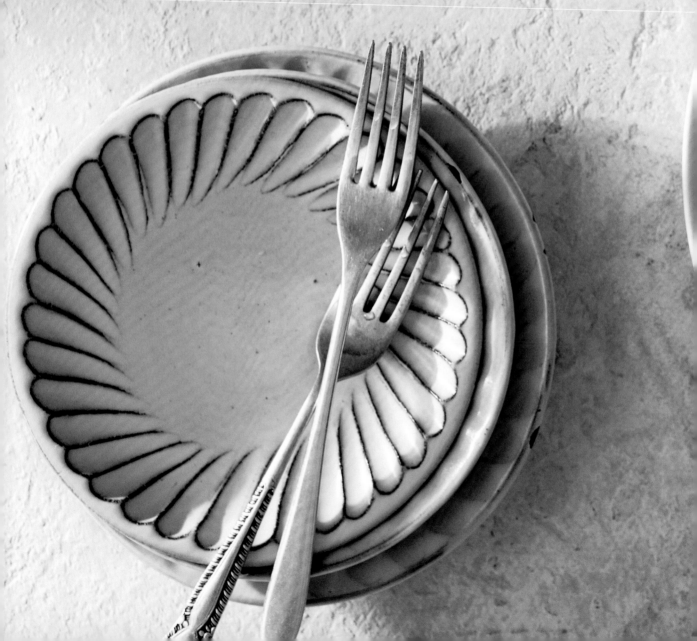

See recipe overleaf

VEGETABLE MAQLUBA

Maqluba means upside down and this savoury rice dish is cooked until set, then turned out and sliced. It also usually contains meat but this version is a great vegetarian or vegan alternative. It's still just as much of a feast – the combination of aubergine, peppers and cauliflower offer a similar texture to the meaty counterparts.

Serves 6

2 medium aubergines, each cut into 6 slices, lengthways
6–7 tbsp olive oil, plus extra for greasing
2 red peppers, cut into 6 slices
1 medium cauliflower, broken into small florets
½ tsp ground turmeric
½ tsp ground coriander
1 tsp ground paprika
1 medium red onion, peeled and sliced
1 garlic clove, peeled and crushed
1 tsp cumin
½ tsp allspice
½ tsp cinnamon
½ tsp mild chilli powder
½ tsp salt
½ tsp ground black pepper
750ml/1 pint 7oz good-quality vegetable stock, hot
1 bay leaf
3 medium tomatoes, sliced
250g/1½ cups basmati rice

Preheat the oven to 200°C fan/425°F/gas mark 7.

Brush the aubergine slices with 1 tablespoon of the oil and lay on a large baking sheet. Season and cook in the oven for 20 minutes, turning halfway and brushing with oil again.

Lay the slices of pepper on one side of a large baking sheet. Brush with 1 tablespoon of the oil and season well.

Put the cauliflower into a bowl with the turmeric, coriander and paprika and 2 tablespoons oil. Season and toss to coat well. Spread out evenly on the other half of the baking sheet.

Put this baking sheet into the oven when you turn the aubergine and cook until all the vegetables are softened and golden.

Meanwhile, heat the remaining 2 tablespoons oil in a large pan on a medium heat. Fry the onion for 5–6 minutes until softened, stirring occasionally.

Stir in the garlic, cumin, allspice and cinnamon, chilli powder, salt and pepper and fry for 1–2 minutes. Add the vegetable stock with the bay leaf and bring to a gentle simmer, for about 5–10 minutes, until it is required.

Grease and line the base of a 20–22cm/8–9in round deep ovenproof dish with baking parchment. Arrange 6 pieces of the roasted aubergine in the bottom of the dish like the spokes of a wheel, with the fatter slices in the middle and the thinner slices up the side of the dish. Alternate with a slice of the pepper in between.

Now, arrange the tomatoes in a single layer to cover the base. Follow with a layer of cauliflower. Sprinkle the rice over evenly.

Pour over the stock and onions. Remove the bay leaf. Lay the remaining aubergine and pepper on top, in spokes again to form a top layer. Tuck in the ends and press down to compress, so that everything is submerged in stock – use a small plate to help.

Cover and cook in the oven for 30 minutes. Remove and leave to stand for 20–30 minutes with the lid on, to allow the rice to continue to cook and firm up, and until it is cool enough to handle.

Take the lid off the pan, put a large serving plate on top and carefully flip over to turn out. Lift off the dish and remove the baking paper. Allow to cool and set a little, then cut into wedges to serve.

SHAMI KABAB

These savoury cakes are made from minced beef and chana dal and resemble little burgers. If you want to prepare ahead, make the mixture up to the point at which it needs to be shaped. Or take it to the next stage where the patties are shaped and they are ready to be fried. Either way, store in the fridge until you're ready to cook.

Serves 4–6

100g/scant ½ cup chana dal,
   soaked in cold water for at
   least 1 hour
1 medium onion,
   roughly chopped
2 garlic cloves, chopped
2cm/¾in piece fresh ginger,
   peeled and roughly chopped
250g/generous 1 cup minced
   beef
1 tsp ground coriander
½ tsp ground turmeric
½ tsp mild chilli powder
½ tsp ground black pepper
½ tsp salt
1 cinnamon stick
handful fresh coriander
   (around 15g/⅓ cup), leaves
   and stalks, roughly torn.
1 tsp garam masala
1 medium egg, beaten
1–2 tbsp plain flour or gram
   flour (or besan flour)
sunflower or vegetable oil,
   for frying

Drain and rinse the chana dal, then put into a large pan. Add the chopped onion, garlic, ginger and minced beef. Break up the mince with a fork and stir in the coriander, turmeric, chilli, black pepper and salt.

Pour over around 300ml/1⅓ cup water to just cover the meat and add the cinnamon stick. Partially cover with a lid and bring to a simmer. Cook for 20 minutes on a medium heat, stirring occasionally. Remove the lid and cook for a further 15–20 minutes, until the chana dal are just tender, all the water has evaporated and the meat is just starting to brown. It's important to drive off as much of the liquid as possible so that the mixture is not too wet and the patties hold together well. Leave to cool for about 15–20 minutes. Remove the cinnamon stick and discard.

Tip the mixture into a food processor. Add the fresh coriander and garam masala. Blend everything to make a smooth paste, scraping down the sides to ensure it is all evenly mixed. Gradually add enough of the egg to bind the mixture without making it too wet. Transfer the mix into a bowl and stir in the flour to give a manageable mixture, that again is not too wet.

To shape the kebabs, wet your hands and divide the mixture into 12 portions. Roll each portion into a ball then flatten to make a pattie about 6cm/2½in in diameter and 1cm/½in thick. Place on a lined tray and repeat with the remaining mixture. Refrigerate for 30 minutes to firm up.

When you are ready to cook the patties, line a plate with kitchen paper. Heat a tablespoon of oil in a large heavy-based frying pan over a medium heat. Fry the patties in batches for 2–3 minutes on each side, or until golden-brown, cooked through and piping hot. Add a little more oil to the pan if needed.

Remove the patties from the pan. Drain on the lined plate and serve immediately with salad and flatbreads.

HAREES

Harees is the wheat and meat porridge that is special for many families at Eid. It consists of barley or wheat berries, simmered with a joint of lamb which slowly infuses its flavour into the grains. It's a humble dish, but with a topping of shredded lamb, crispy onions and a drizzle of ghee, it becomes a feast.

Serves 6, generously

400g/2 cups pearl barley or
    wheat berries – you will need
    to soak this overnight first
1kg/2¼lb shoulder of lamb,
    bone-in
1 tsp ground cardamom
1 large tbsp ghee, melted
salt and pepper

Pour the barley or wheat berries into a sieve and rinse well. Tip into a large bowl, cover with water and leave to soak overnight.

The next day, drain the barley or wheat berries thoroughly.

Pour 3 litres/5¼ pints water into a very large pan and bring to the boil. Pour in the soaked barley or wheat berries and cook for 45 minutes. Lower the lamb into the water, reduce the heat to a very low simmer and continue to cook for 2–3 hours until the meat is very tender.

Add the cardamom and season to taste with salt and pepper. Continue to cook for a further 20 minutes.

Take the pan off the heat. Lift the meat out of the pan and shred it, discarding the bone. Use a hand blender to blitz the mixture to a porridge-like consistency. Drizzle over the ghee before serving.

> *Cook's tip*
> *For a special topping, dress the harees with toasted cashew nuts, fresh coriander and freshly cooked crispy onions (see lentil soup recipe on page 46).*

SPICED LAMB AND CHICKPEA TART

Here, gently spiced minced lamb and chickpeas are arranged on a puff-pastry base, drizzled with a hummus dressing and fresh mint. This is perfect served with a simple salad made with deseeded cucumber, thin slivers of red onion and mint leaves and dressed with a squeeze of lemon juice.

Serves 6

For the tart
2 tsp olive oil
1 red onion, finely chopped
500g/2 cups lean minced lamb
1 large carrot, coarsely grated
1 tsp ground cumin
1 tsp ground coriander
pinch of ground cinnamon
4 cardamom pods, crushed and
   seeds finely ground
2 tbsp tomato purée
salt and ground black pepper
1 large tomato, roughly chopped
320g/11oz puff pastry
400g/14oz can chickpeas
2 tbsp freshly chopped
   flat-leaf parsley
2 tbsp freshly chopped coriander

For the hummus drizzle
90g/½ cup chickpeas (the
   remaining chickpeas
2 tsp tahini
¼ garlic clove
1 tbsp lemon juice
2 tbsp olive oil
¼ tsp ground cumin

To serve
fresh mint leaves
cucumber salad, if liked

Preheat the oven to 180°C fan/400°F/gas mark 6. First make the meat filling. Heat the oil in a saucepan, add the onion and cook for 7–8 minutes, stirring occasionally over a medium heat until the onion has softened.

Increase the heat, then add the lamb, stirring to break up the larger pieces. Continue to cook for 5–10 minutes to brown the lamb, then stir in the grated carrot. Sprinkle all the spices over the lamb, season well and add the tomato purée. Cook for 2 minutes, stirring continuously.

Now add the chopped tomato, cover and cook for 10–15 minutes until the lamb is completely cooked. (Add a splash of water if it's a little dry.)

While the lamb is cooking, bake the pastry case. Unroll the pastry and place onto a baking sheet using the parchment it came on to line the baking sheet. Using a small sharp knife, carefully score a 1cm/½in border around the edge. Take care not to cut the pastry all the way through. Bake in the oven for 20–25 minutes until the pastry is cooked through and golden brown.

Drain the chickpeas and when the lamb is cooked, stir in 150g/¾ cup of the chickpeas (save the remaining 90g/½ cup for the hummus). Remove from the heat, then stir in the fresh parsley and coriander, season to taste and keep warm.

Remove the pastry from the oven and, using the back of a spoon, press the centre of the pastry down to create a case for your lamb. Spoon the meat filling into the centre. Transfer back to the oven for 10 minutes to heat through.

Now make the hummus drizzle. Whizz all the ingredients in a food processor with 1–2 tablespoons cold water. Taste, then add seasoning and add a little water to thin the houmous. You may need to add a little more water – it needs to be pourable.

Remove the tart from the oven and serve straightaway, drizzled with the hummus. Sprinkle with fresh mint leaves and serve with a cucumber salad for a bit of crunch if you like.

MARGOUGA AL DAJAJ

This wonderfully aromatic chicken stew brings together all the signature Emirati spices with chicken and fresh vegetables. There's no stock used here, just water for the base and dried lemons which infuse their musky flavour into the stew as it cooks.

Serves 4

45g/3 tbsp ghee
1 small red onion,
  chopped finely
6 garlic cloves, chopped
300g/1½ cups tomatoes
  (around 2 large tomatoes),
  chopped
1 tbsp local spices – use 1 tsp
  each cumin, mild chilli
  powder and freshly ground
  black pepper
¾ tsp ground turmeric
200g/7oz skinless, boneless
  chicken (thigh or breast),
  chopped into 2cm/¾in pieces
1 small potato, chopped
  into cubes
1 small carrot, cut into batons
1 small courgette,
  cut into batons
2 dried lemons, pierced a
  couple of times
salt, to taste
300g/10oz Emirate regag bread
  or wholemeal flatbread,
  roughly torn

To serve
small handful freshly
  chopped coriander

Put the ghee into a large saucepan and melt over a medium heat.

Add the onion, garlic and tomatoes and stir into the ghee. Turn down the heat a little and continue to sauté the mixture until the onions have softened and the tomatoes have cooked down to a pulp, around 7–8 minutes.

Stir in the spices, chicken and chopped vegetables, tossing them all in the tomato base until well coated and then cooking for 2–3 minutes.

Pour in 800ml/3½ cups of boiling water, add the dried lemons and a good seasoning of salt.

Cover the pan and bring to a simmer. Cook for 40–45 minutes until the chicken is tender and the sauce has reduced and thickened. Stir every now and then so that the vegetables don't stick to the base of the pan.

Stir the regag bread into the gravy and cook over a low heat until the bread is soft.

Spoon into bowls and serve straightaway, garnished with coriander.

See recipes overleaf

TABBOULEH

This simple herb salad is a great partner to grilled fish or meat. If you have friends for supper, this recipe makes enough to serve in a small bowl as an appetiser, alongside the hummus and moutabel (opposite and page 40) and some flatbread. Double the recipe if you'd like to serve it as a side salad.

Serves 4–6, as an appetiser

2 tbsp bulgar wheat

2 tbsp boiling water

60g/1⅓ cup flat-leaf parsley, chopped finely

10g/⅓ cup mint sprigs, leaves pulled and finely chopped

¼ small red onion, finely chopped

1 small tomato (about 100g/ ½ cup), deseeded and finely chopped

4 tbsp mild-flavoured extra virgin olive oil

juice of ½ lemon

a pinch each of ground cumin, ground coriander and sumac

salt and freshly ground black pepper

First put the bulgar wheat into a bowl and pour over 2 tablespoons boiling water, then set aside.

Add the parsley, mint, red onion and tomato. Stir everything together. Whisk the olive oil, lemon juice and spices together in a bowl and season. Taste to check the seasoning and adjust if necessary, then stir into the herb mixture. Set the bowl aside for 1 hour before serving.

HUMMUS

No table is complete without hummus. Here, bicarbonate of soda is added to the water when cooking the chickpeas, which helps to break down and soften their skins, making them easy to remove after cooking. It's well worth making the effort to do this as it gives the hummus a really smooth, creamy texture.

Serves 4–6

125g/⅝ cup dried chickpeas, soaked in a bowl of cold water overnight
½ tsp bicarbonate of soda
3 garlic cloves, peeled, left whole
3 tbsp tahini
2–3 tbsp strained lemon juice, to taste
¾ tsp salt
¾ tsp cumin seeds, toasted and finely ground

For scattering and drizzling over:
piece of roasted red pepper in oil (from a jar, drained), diced
a handful of toasted pine nuts
extra-virgin olive oil

Drain the chickpeas and tip into a large saucepan. Add the bicarbonate of soda and 1 litre/scant 4½ cups of cold water, bring to the boil and bubble well for 10 minutes. Reduce the heat, add the garlic and simmer for 30 minutes or until tender. Skim any froth as it rises to the surface. To check the chickpeas are ready, press one between your fingers – it should be soft and break down easily.

Strain 2 tablespoons of cooking liquid from the chickpeas, then drain them. Set aside the garlic. Tip the chickpeas into a big bowl and cover with cold water. Rub the chickpeas between your hands. Most of the skins should float to the surface, so scoop them up and discard. Drain and repeat with fresh water until you have removed most of the skins. Drain well.

Put the chickpeas in a food processor. Roughly chop the reserved garlic and add to the processor bowl with the reserved cooking liquid. Process until smooth, then add the tahini, lemon juice, salt and ½ teaspoon of the ground cumin. Process for 2–3 minutes until the hummus is very smooth and creamy.

Serve the hummus in small bowls, scattered with the diced red pepper, toasted pine nuts, the remaining cumin and a drizzle of oil.

DINNER

Lunch is never enough on its own
at Eid. Dinner brings a change of
menu, new visitors and the start of
the close of the celebration.

GRILLED VEGETABLE KEBABS

There's a lovely creamy taste to these delicately spiced vegetables, thanks to the melted butter in the marinade. For a vegetarian feast, team with the lentil pilaf and the kohlrabi and carrot salad on the side. When you're preparing for a crowd, prepare all veg and marinate them beforehand, so that there's less to do on the day.

Makes 6 large skewers

6 new potatoes
375g/2½ cups butternut
    squash, peeled
    and cut into 8–12 pieces
1 red pepper, cut into 12 pieces
1 large courgette, cut into
    12 slices
6 chestnut mushrooms, cleaned
12 bay leaves

For the marinade
2 tsp ground cumin
2 tsp ground coriander
zest and juice of 1 lemon
1 pinch saffron
25g/¼ stick unsalted butter,
    melted
4 tbsp olive oil
salt and black pepper

Lemon wedges, to serve

Soak 6 large wooden skewers in water for 20 minutes (or use metal ones). Bring a pan of water to the boil and boil the potatoes for 15 minutes until just tender. Add the butternut squash after 5 minutes. When the potatoes and squash are just cooked, drain well and tip into a bowl.

Add the peppers, courgettes and mushrooms to the potatoes and squash.

Mix together the ingredients for the marinade and pour over all the vegetables. Stir well and set aside for at least 1 hour, or overnight in the fridge.

When you're ready to cook, preheat the grill to its highest setting. Thread alternate vegetables onto the soaked wooden skewers with the bay leaves. Season with a little salt and pepper and grill for 8–10 minutes, turning regularly until the vegetables are cooked through and beginning to brown on the edges.

Serve hot, with lemon wedges.

Cook's tip
These delicately spiced vegetable kebabs are delicious on their own but you can also serve them with a garlic dip. Simply mix together 4 tablespoons each of mayonnaise and low-fat Greek yogurt, stir in a little grated garlic, if you like, to taste, and season with salt and pepper.

TRADITIONAL VEGETABLE SALONA

This recipe is a wonderful celebration of simple vegetables with aromatic spices. The stew is simmered for just under 30 minutes, so that the vegetables still hold their shape, but are lovely and tender.

Serves 4

50g/3¼ tbsp ghee
50g/⅓ cup red onion, chopped
   (about ½ small red onion)
3 garlic cloves, finely chopped
200g/1 cup tomatoes, chopped
   (about 2 medium tomatoes)
½ tsp crushed black
   peppercorns
1 tsp ground coriander
¼ tsp ground cumin
¼ tsp chilli powder
1 cinnamon stick
½ tsp turmeric powder
a good pinch ground cinnamon
½ tsp ground cardamom
500ml/generous 2 cups water
1 tsp tomato purée
400g/ scant 2½ cups potatoes,
   peeled and chopped into
   2–3cm/¾–1¼in chunks
300g/2 cups baby marrow or
   courgette, chopped into
   2–3cm/¾–1¼ in chunks
2 dried lemons

To serve
a good handful of
   chopped fresh coriander
steamed basmati rice
   or flatbread

Heat the ghee in a large saucepan over a medium heat, stir in the onion, garlic and tomatoes and sauté for 6–8 minutes, stirring often until the onion has softened and the tomatoes become saucy.

Add the black pepper, ground coriander, cumin, chilli powder, cinnamon stick, turmeric, ground cinnamon and cardamom, and cook for 1 minute until fragrant.

Gradually pour in the water, stirring all the time. Add the tomato purée, potato and baby marrow or courgette and the dried lemons. Bring to a gentle simmer and cook, uncovered, for about 25–30 minutes, until the vegetables are cooked but still keep their shape.

Scoop out the dried lemons and cut each in half. Spoon the stew into bowls and finish with a sprinkling of chopped coriander and half a dried lemon for each bowl. Serve with rice or bread.

Cook's tip
If you can't get hold of dried lemons, use 1 preserved lemon and cut into quarters. Serve one for each bowl.

RICE AND LENTIL PILAF

This is a wonderful dish to enjoy on its own, but it's also brilliant as part of a feast as it can be dressed up or down depending on what you have to hand. Here, a handful of chopped coriander adds freshness to the finished dish, but you could add pine nuts, browned in a little ghee or butter, and a few jewel-like pomegranate seeds.

Serves 4–6

6 tbsp olive oil

3 medium onions, halved and finely sliced

1 tsp brown sugar

150g/⅔ cup green lentils, washed

200g/1 cup basmati rice

1 tsp ground cumin

1 tsp ground coriander

1 tsp ground cinnamon

½ tsp ground allspice

½ tsp turmeric

½ tsp salt

2 tbsp freshly chopped coriander

Heat 3 tablespoons oil in a frying pan and cook the onions over a low heat for 30–40 minutes, stirring often, until deep golden brown in colour. Stir in the sugar and cook for a minute, then remove the onions to a plate lined with kitchen paper.

Put the lentils into a pan and cover with cold water. Bring to the boil and cook until almost tender – about 30 minutes. While the lentils are cooking, soak the rice in cold water for 20 minutes.

Heat the remaining oil in a deep, lidded frying pan. Add all the spices and the salt and stir together, cooking for around 1 minute.

Drain the rice and add to the pan. Cook for 2–3 minutes, stirring the rice so it becomes coated in the spice mixture. Add 400ml/generous 1⅔ cups water and bring to the boil. Cover and reduce the heat. Cook for about 10 minutes.

Drain the lentils and add to the rice. Cover and heat through, still on a very low heat, for 5 minutes.

Remove the pan from the heat, and stir in the onions and coriander, and serve.

'As children visit the homes of relatives to congratulate them on the holiday, they're given a sum of money called "Eidyah", to help teach them the value of money from a young age.'

VEGETABLE BERYANI

Here's a twist on our favourite beryani dish but, instead of featuring meat or fish, it's a vegetarian version. It combines pepper, squash and red onion, roasted until tender, which are then tossed in a richly spiced masala gravy with chickpeas – and it's delicious. If you want to make it vegan, use olive oil in the masala gravy.

Serves 4–6

For the rice and vegetables

300g/1½ cups long basmati rice
400g/2⅔ cups squash, chopped
1 medium red pepper, deseeded
  and chopped into pieces
1 medium red onion, chopped
1 tbsp olive oil
a pinch of ground coriander
a pinch of ground turmeric
salt and black pepper
25g/scant ¼ cup whole roasted,
  salted mixed nuts
1 lemon, cut into wedges

For the masala gravy

2 tbsp olive oil or ghee,
  plus extra to brush
1 small onion, finely chopped
1½ tsp ground coriander
¾ tsp ground cinnamon
seeds from 4 cardamom pods,
  finely ground with ½ tsp salt
1 bay leaf
1 green chilli, chopped
2 garlic cloves, crushed
5cm/2in fresh ginger, grated
400g/2 cups tomatoes, chopped
30g/⅝ cup coriander, chopped,
  plus extra to garnish
400g/14oz can chickpeas,
  drained

Preheat the oven to 200°C fan/425°F/gas mark 7. Line a large roasting tin with baking parchment.

Pour the rice into a bowl, pour over 900ml/1 pint 12 fl oz cold water and stir in 1 teaspoon salt. Set aside to soak.

Put all the chopped vegetables into the tin and pour over the olive oil. Season with the spices and salt and pepper and toss everything together well. Roast for 20–25 minutes until just tender and golden.

Pour the water and rice into a large saucepan and cover. Bring to the boil, then reduce the heat to the lowest setting and cook for 6 minutes. Drain well.

While the rice is boiling, heat the oil or ghee in a pan over a medium heat. As soon as it's heated, stir in the onion and cook for 5–8 minutes, stirring every now and then, until the onions are golden and starting to soften. Add the coriander, cinnamon, ground cardamom, season and cook for 1–2 minutes. Add 2 tablespoons water and cook until it looks like a paste.

Add the bay leaf, chilli, garlic and ginger and continue to cook for a few more minutes to cook off the garlic. Stir in the tomatoes and season, then cover the pan and turn down the heat. Cook for 5–7 minutes until the tomatoes have cooked down and thickened and the whole mixture looks like a thick gravy. Stir in the coriander and take off the heat.

As soon as the roasted vegetables come out of the oven, reduce the heat to 180°C fan/400°F/gas mark 6. Take a wide casserole pan and brush with a little oil or ghee. Spoon in half the rice and cover the base. Add the vegetables and drained chickpeas to the masala gravy and stir, then spoon on the first layer of rice. Cover with the remaining rice and put a lid on the pan. Transfer to the oven and cook for 20–25 minutes until completely hot.

Spoon onto plates and garnish with the coriander, nuts and lemon wedges.

KEEMA PARATHA

There's a delicious nutty flavour to these minced beef flatbreads, thanks to the wholemeal flour used in the dough. The secret to the crisp and flaky pastry is to roll the dough out several times, spreading it with ghee each time so that it creates layers that become laminated by the time the rounds are fried.

Makes 8

For the paratha
450g/4 cups wholemeal plain
　flour, plus extra for dusting
2 tsp salt
200ml/scant 1 cup warm water
2 tbsp oil or ghee, melted and
　cooled, plus extra for
　brushing, frying and greasing

For the filling
1 small onion, roughly chopped
2 tsp grated fresh ginger
1 garlic clove, peeled
1 tbsp oil
2 tsp tomato purée
1 tsp ground cumin
1 tsp ground coriander
¼ tsp ground clove
¼ tsp ground nutmeg
½ tsp freshly ground
　black pepper
¼ tsp salt
200g/scant 1 cup beef mince

Put the flour and salt into a bowl and add the water, oil or ghee. Bring together to a soft dough and knead for 5 minutes. Add up to 50ml/3⅓ tablespoons water if the dough doesn't come together. Put in a greased bowl, cover, set aside for 1 hour.

Make the filling. Put the onion, ginger and garlic into a small food processor and blitz to a paste. Scrape down the sides frequently until it is fairly smooth.

Heat the oil in a frying pan. When hot, add the onion paste and fry for 3–4 minutes, stirring occasionally until starting to soften. Add the tomato purée and spices, pepper and salt and stir-fry for another 1–2 minutes.

Now add the beef mince to the pan. Stir to break up the pieces and make sure the mince is well coated with the spice paste. Cook for 6–8 minutes over a medium heat until browned with no traces of pink. Cover and set aside to cool.

After the paratha dough has been rising for an hour, divide it into 8 pieces. Roll each piece out on a floured worktop as thinly as possible, to around 16–18cm/ 6¼–7in in diameter. Brush a small amount of softened ghee or oil over the surface, then roll it up so that the fat is on the inside of the dough.

Roll it again from each end so that it forms an 'S' shaped spiral that meets in the middle, then fold one half on top of the other half to make a round. Roll this out flat to around 12cm/5in wide. This will help to laminate the dough to form layers and keep it crisp and flaky. Put 1–2 tablespoons of the filling into the centre of each circle and draw the sides over, pinching to seal in the centre. Roll out on a floured worktop as thinly as possible to around 16cm/6¼in wide, ensuring that the filling doesn't break through.

Heat a drizzle of oil or a knob of ghee in a large frying pan. Cook each paratha for 2–3 minutes on each side, until crisp and golden and cooked through. Spread a little more ghee or oil over the top to glaze and add flavour. Keep warm while you finish rolling and frying the remaining parathas. Serve immediately.

SPICED LAMB KEBABS

The mix of spices is what makes these lamb kebabs extra special. It's best if you can leave the marinade on for as long as possible, to allow the flavours to infuse the meat. Take care not to overcook the lamb or the meat will be tough – it should still be slightly pink inside and lovely and tender within.

Serves 4

600g/1¼lb lean boned lamb,
    cut into 2cm/¾in cubes

For the marinade
2 garlic cloves, crushed
    and chopped
1 tsp ground coriander
1 tsp ground cumin
1 tbsp garam masala
¼ tsp ground turmeric
a good pinch of chilli powder,
    optional
2.5cm/1in piece root ginger,
    peeled and grated
1 tbsp olive oil
salt and freshly ground
    black pepper

To serve
flatbread, sliced onion,
    tomatoes, yogurt

Put all the marinade ingredients into a bowl and combine together thoroughly. Add the lamb and mix well, making sure all the pieces of meat are coated. Cover and leave in the fridge for at least 2 hours, but longer if possible.

When you are ready to cook, soak 8 wooden skewers in warm water for 20 minutes, or use metal skewers.

Thread the lamb onto the skewers and cook on a hot griddle or barbecue for 12–15 minutes, turning frequently.

Serve with the flatbread, sliced onion, tomatoes and yogurt.

MUTTON AND LENTIL HALEEM STEW

This rich dish of lentils cooked slowly with meat was a favourite in the court of the Mughal Emperor Akbar. When I was growing up, haleem signaled celebration – it was the centrepiece of any feast in our home. I would save my appetite for this, devouring it with lemon juice, ginger, fried onions and warm naan bread. What a treat...

Serves 8

100ml/scant ½ cup olive oil

1 onion, thinly sliced

500g/18oz boneless mutton, cubed

3 garlic cloves, finely grated

1 tbsp grated ginger

1–2 tsp chilli powder

1 tsp cracked black pepper

1 tsp ground cumin

1 tsp ground coriander

1 tsp garam masala

½ tsp turmeric

100g/scant ½ cup chana dal (yellow split lentils)

100g/scant ½ cup moong/mung dal (huskless split mung beans)

100g/scant ½ cup masoor dal (red lentils)

100g/scant ½ cup urad dal (white huskless black gram lentils)

100g/½ cup pearl barley

4 litres/7 pints warm water

salt, to taste

To garnish

handful of ready-made crispy fried onions

handful of fresh coriander

fresh ginger, peeled and cut into julienne

lemon wedges

I use a pressure cooker to make my haleem. If you don't have one, you can prepare it as below using a large heavy-based pan instead, although you will need to cook it for about 4–5 hours to get the same deliciously soft texture.

Pour the oil into a pressure cooker and place over a medium heat. Once the oil is hot, add the sliced onion and fry until it is a deep golden brown. Add the mutton cubes to the pan, followed by the garlic, ginger and all the spices. Stir for a few minutes to coat the meat in the spices.

Once the meat has started to colour, add all the lentils, pearl barley and the water, season with salt and bring to the boil. If your pressure cooker won't take all the water, pour in as much as you can, then once the stew is cooked, take the lid off and add the remainder and bring to a simmer to heat through.

Put the lid of the pressure cooker on the pan; when the pressure starts whistling, reduce the heat to medium and leave to cook in the pressure cooker for 2 hours. Every 30 minutes or so pick up the entire pressure cooker (wearing oven gloves) and swirl it around gently to redistribute the ingredients.

When the time is up, remove the pressure cooker from the heat and allow to cool. Carefully remove the lid and stir the contents vigorously with a wooden spoon to break down the meat fibres and combine them with the lentils. Season with salt to taste. The final texture should be that of a thick, textured soup – if you prefer a thinner texture, add a little hot water.

Serve the haleem in deep bowls, garnished with crispy fried onions, fresh coriander, julienned ginger and lemon wedges with some flatbread.

LAMB THAREED

This classic Emirati stew is a wonderful one-pot and is infused with spices and the musky flavour of dried lemon. Keep the lamb in large pieces so that it doesn't shrivel up when cooked.

Serves 4

50g/3⅓ tbsp ghee
1 medium red onion, chopped
6 garlic cloves, chopped
400g/2 cups just-ripe tomatoes,
    roughly chopped
500g/18oz boneless lamb
    shoulder, chopped into
    3cm/1¼in cubes
1 small potato, chopped
1 small carrot, chopped
    into batons
1 small courgette,
    chopped into batons
10g local spices (use 1 tsp each
    freshly ground black pepper,
    chilli powder and ground
    cumin)
¼ tsp ground turmeric
2 dried lemons, pierced a
    couple of times
500ml/generous 2 cups
    hot water
4–5 pieces of Emirate regag
    bread or wholemeal flatbread,
    torn into pieces
salt, to season

To serve
a few sprigs of fresh coriander,
    optional

Heat the ghee in a deep saucepan over a low heat. As soon as it's melted, stir in the onion, garlic and tomatoes. Stir everything together and cook over a medium heat for 5 minutes until starting to soften.

Stir in the lamb, vegetables, spices and dried lemons, and season with salt. Stir everything together and cook for a couple of minutes, then pour in the hot water.

Cover the pan and bring to the boil. Reduce the heat to its lowest setting and simmer for 40–50 minutes, until the lamb is tender.

Arrange the pieces of bread among four plates and spoon over the meat, vegetables and broth, letting the bread gradually absorb the broth.

Serve with a few sprigs of fresh coriander.

See recipe overleaf

RAAN MUSSALLUM

The pre-marinade helps to tenderise this leg of lamb. The full marinade of yogurt and papaya cut with spices and extra garlic and ginger, works its magic over a couple of days. Use the cooked masala to make an amazing pulao (see tip at the end) to serve alongside and throw in a portion of French fries and salad to complete the meal.

Serves 6

1¼–1½kg/3–3lb 5oz leg of goat or lamb, cleaned and trimmed of any fat

For the pre-marinade
1 tsp salt
1 tsp freshly ground black pepper
1 tbsp lemon juice
1 tsp garlic paste
1 tsp ginger paste

For the marinade
2 medium onions, finely chopped
2 tbsp sunflower oil, plus extra for drizzling
500g/2 cups full-fat Greek yogurt
4 tbsp raw papaya purée (you'll need around 75g/ ½ cup fruit, peeled)
1 small bunch of coriander, chopped, plus extra to garnish
3 tbsp tomato purée
2 tsp mild chilli powder
¼ tsp ground turmeric

Put the leg of goat or lamb on a board. Mix the pre-marinade ingredients together in a bowl, then rub all over the meat. Set aside for 20 minutes.

Make the marinade. Put the onions into a pan with the sunflower oil. Stir together and cook over a medium heat for 5–8 minutes until they start to turn golden. Spoon into a bowl to cool.

Mix the yogurt and papaya purée together in a bowl. Add the coriander, tomato purée, chilli, turmeric, cumin seeds, lemon juice, olive oil, ginger and garlic pastes, tandoori masala spice mix and the green chillies and season well. Stir in the cooled, sautéed onions.

Rinse the pre-marinade off the leg and pat dry, then put the leg back on the board and use a sharp knife to make deep slits all over the leg. Smother the marinade paste all over the meat. Cover and chill for at least 24 hours and for up to 2 days.

When you're ready to roast the meat, preheat the oven to 150°C fan/325°F/ gas mark 3.

Heat a very large frying pan (or use a heatproof roasting tin) over a medium heat with a drizzle of oil. Scrape off and reserve as much marinade as possible, then lift the joint into the pan and cook for around 10 minutes on each side to colour the meat. Now add the reserved marinade and cook until the oil separates.

Lift the meat into a large baking tray. If it's already in one, you'll need to lift the meat out and put on a board briefly for this stage. Add the soaked cashews and couscous to the pan and cook for 3–5 minutes over a low heat. Spoon the masala on top of the meat (or return it to the tin) and spread all over. Add the warm water to the tray, cover the whole thing with foil and transfer to the oven to roast for 1½–2 hours, depending on the size of the joint.

2 tsp cumin seeds

juice of 1 lemon

2 tbsp olive oil

1 tbsp ginger paste

1 tbsp garlic paste

2 tsp tandoori masala spice mix

4–5 mild green chillies,
    deseeded and chopped

300ml/1⅓ cups warm water

salt and freshly ground
    black pepper

10 cashew nuts, soaked in a bowl
    of cold water

2 tbsp couscous, soaked in a
    bowl with 3 tbsp cold water

After 1 hour, take the tray out of the oven and remove the foil. There will be lots of gravy in the tray. Spoon as much as possible into a bowl so it can be used to make the rice (see tip, below).

When the meat is cooked, preheat the grill. Lift it onto a shallow roasting tin and grill for 5–7 minutes until it's nice and golden. Keep a close eye on it though as the masala can burn in no time at this stage.

Lift onto a warm serving dish and serve with French fries, salad and the pulao, below.

Cook's tip
For the pulao, put the reserved masala into a large pan and stir in 200g/1 cup long basmati rice. Place the pan over a medium heat and stir together for 1–2 minutes. Season well. Pour over 500ml/scant 2 cups warm water, stirring again to mix the rice mixture with the water. Cover and bring to a simmer. Turn the heat down low and cook for 10–12 minutes until steamed through.

LAMB GHOUZI

Traditionally this recipe is made from a range of different joints – goat, beef, lamb as here and, in traditional countries, also camel. You can dress it with nuts and herbs, and even include hard-boiled eggs tucked into the rice. It's often served piled high on platters, which are placed in the middle of the table so everyone can help themselves.

Serves 6, generously

2 shoulders of lamb, bone in
4 tbsp ghee or butter, melted
    and cooled but still runny,
    plus extra to finish
3 tbsp tomato purée
6 garlic cloves, crushed
1 tbsp ground coriander
1½ tbsp ground cumin
juice of 2 lemons
1½ tsp salt
1½ tsp freshly ground
    black pepper
8 small courgettes,
    halved lengthways
8 long thin aubergines,
    halved lengthways
3 large red peppers, halved
8 small carrots,
    halved lengthways
2 tbsp olive oil, plus extra to
    drizzle
25g/⅛ cup pine nuts, toasted
small handful of freshly
    chopped parsley

For the rice
400g/2 cups long basmati rice
½ tsp ground turmeric
1 cinnamon stick
4 whole cloves

Preheat the oven to 160°C fan/350°F/gas mark 4.

Put the lamb shoulders into a large, deep roasting tin and use a small sharp knife to push holes in the meat. Put the ghee or butter into a small bowl and add the tomato purée, garlic, coriander, cumin, lemon juice, salt and pepper. Mix together then roughly divide the mix and spoon half on each shoulder. Spread the paste so it covers the top of each shoulder, rubbing a little into each of the cuts. Pour in 1 litre/generous 4½ cups cold water to the tin and cover with foil. Roast for 3½ hours or until very tender.

After 3 hours, uncover the lamb and put the prepared courgettes, aubergines, peppers and carrots into the base of the pan. Drizzle with 2 tablespoons oil and season well and continue to roast for 30 more minutes until tender.

While the vegetables are cooking, pour the basmati rice into a sieve and rinse well. Pour into a pan and add the ground turmeric, cinnamon and cloves. Add 800ml/3½ cups cold water. Cover the pan and bring to the boil. As soon as the water is boiling, reduce the heat to its lowest setting and cook for 10–12 minutes until the rice is cooked through. Take the pan off the hob and set aside, without lifting the lid, while the lamb finishes cooking.

Heat a knob of butter and drizzle of oil in a pan over a medium heat. Toast the pine nuts until golden and season well.

Spoon the rice onto a very large platter (or use two platters if you need to) and place the lamb shoulders on top. Arrange the vegetables around the outside, then scatter over the pine nuts and parsley. Strain most of the fat from the juices in the pan and pour the juices into a jug or bowl to serve alongside.

CHICKEN MACHBOOS

This spiced one-pot dish combines delicate basmati rice with whole joints of chicken and is rich with spices. It's important to use the chicken with its bones and skin as this contributes to the overall taste. Dried limes are cooked in the rice and are the prized part of this dish. Slice it roughly into four and serve a piece with each portion.

Serves 4

1 tbsp vegetable oil

1kg/2¼lb chicken pieces (bone-in, skin on), i.e. thighs, legs

salt and freshly ground black pepper

2 tbsp ghee

1 medium red onion, chopped

1 medium white onion, chopped

1 cinnamon stick

2 dried limes, pierced 3–4 times

1 plump green chilli, seeds removed if liked, finely chopped

1 tbsp grated fresh root ginger

1 tbsp grated or crushed garlic

1½ tsp ground cumin

1 tsp turmeric

1 tsp paprika

½ tsp ground coriander

½ tsp ground cinnamon

½ tsp ground cardamom (or crushed seeds)

pinch each of ground cloves and nutmeg

2 medium tomatoes, chopped

600–650ml/2⅔–scant 3 cups hot chicken stock

280g/scant 1½ cups basmati rice

2 tbsp fresh coriander, chopped, plus extra to garnish

Heat the oil in a large sauté pan. Season the chicken pieces with a little salt and pepper and fry over a medium–high heat for about 5–7 minutes, until browned all over. Do this in 2 batches if necessary, as you don't want to crowd the pan. Remove chicken to a plate and set aside. Discard all but 2 tablespoons of oil from the pan.

Melt the ghee in the same pan. Add the onions, cinnamon stick and limes and fry over a medium–high heat until the onions start to turn brown, about 8–9 minutes, stirring occasionally. Stir in the green chilli, grated ginger and garlic and stir-fry for 2 minutes. Mix in the ground spices and stir-fry for 1–2 minutes until fragrant. Add the tomatoes and cook on a medium heat until they have softened, about 3–4 minutes. Stir in ¾ teaspoon salt and a good pinch of pepper.

Slowly pour 500ml/generous 2 cups of the stock into the pan, stirring and scraping up any bits from the bottom of the pan as you do so. Sit the chicken pieces back in the pan, skin-side up, so they are about three quarters submerged in liquid. Bring to a gentle simmer, cover the pan and continue to simmer on a low heat for about 50 minutes to one hour, or until the chicken is tender. Tip the rice into a bowl, cover with cold water and leave to soak.

Stir the coriander into the pan. Drain the rice, then stir the rice into the pan with another 100ml/scant ½ cup of the stock. Bring to a boil, then lower the heat, cover and simmer for a further 15 minutes or until the rice is cooked and has absorbed the liquid. Check and stir occasionally. If more liquid is required, add enough of the remaining stock to finish cooking the rice. Remove from the heat and leave covered for 5 minutes for the rice to fluff up. Serve scattered with extra fresh coriander.

CHICKEN KEBABS WITH YOGURT DRESSING

This recipe calls for minced chicken which is easy to do in a food processor. Choose good-quality plump breasts or thighs, or a mixture, and remove any fat or sinew before processing. The dressing recipe makes plenty – leftovers can be stored in the fridge for up to three days. Get everyone involved in helping to shape the pieces.

Serves 4–6

For the kebabs
1 medium onion, chopped into chunks
4 garlic cloves
750g/1lb 10oz skinless, boneless chicken, minced
1 large egg, beaten
1 tsp grated fresh ginger
15g/⅓ cup fresh breadcrumbs
1 tsp ground cumin
1 tsp ground coriander
1 tsp mild red chilli powder
1 tsp garam masala
½ tsp turmeric
1 tsp salt
juice of ½ lemon
2 tbsp olive oil

For the yogurt dressing
½ medium-sized onion, chopped into chunks
200g/scant 1 cup Greek yogurt
juice of 2 limes
1 bunch of fresh coriander (about 25g/½ cup), plus extra to garnish
1 tsp extra virgin olive oil
¼ tsp salt
1 tsp black pepper

In a mini food processor, blitz the onion and garlic into a smooth paste. Scrape down the sides every now and then to help make it as smooth as possible.

Put the minced chicken into a large bowl, then add the onion and garlic paste, the egg, ginger, breadcrumbs, cumin, coriander, red chilli, garam masala, turmeric, salt and the lemon juice. Mix the ingredients together to combine.

Cover with clingfilm and leave to marinate in the fridge for at least 1 hour or overnight.

When you're ready to cook, make the yogurt dressing. In a food processor, blitz the onion to form a smooth paste. Pour in the yogurt and the lime juice, then add the coriander, 1 teaspoon olive oil, salt and pepper. Whizz together until combined.

With wet hands, divide the chicken mixture into 8 large meatballs or 12 smaller ones and flatten in the palm of your hand to form a disc around 2.5cm/1in thick. Wash your hands after handling raw chicken.

Heat a large griddle pan over a medium–high heat. Pour the oil into the pan.

Gently place the meatballs into the hot pan and cook for 4–5 minutes until golden brown on each side and cooked through, with no trace of pink inside. Cook in batches if necessary. Transfer to a plate and drain on kitchen paper.

Serve hot with the dressing, garnished with the extra coriander. It goes well with some salad and bread.

ARSEEYAH

This simple rice and chicken stew is a classic Eid recipe, which is served for dinner and is loved by all. A simple stock is made by cooking pieces of chicken, bones included, and used to cook rice until tender, which is then whizzed together until smooth. The dish is quite thick, almost porridge-like, and is very filling, too.

Serves 4–6

4 chicken thighs, (around
   600g/1¼lb)
4 whole cloves
1 cinnamon stick
1 bay leaf
125g/generous ½ cup
   short-grain rice
¼ tsp ground cardamom
salt and freshly ground
   black pepper
25g/¼ stick salted butter,
   chopped

To serve, optional
2 tbsp ready-fried onions

Put the chicken in a large saucepan and pour over 1.5 litres/2½ pints cold water. Add the cloves, cinnamon stick and bay leaf. Bring to a simmer then reduce the heat to low and cook for 30 minutes until the chicken is very tender.

Strain the stock into a large bowl. Discard the spices then pick the chicken off the bone and discard the bones.

Pour the stock back into the pan and add the short-grain rice, the cardamom and the chicken strips. Season well. Bring to a boil and simmer for 15 minutes until the rice is soft.

When the rice has finished cooking, blend the whole mixture until smooth. Reheat until piping hot, stirring often.

Divide the mixture among warm serving bowls, dot each with a little butter so it melts over the rice, and top with the ready-fried onions.

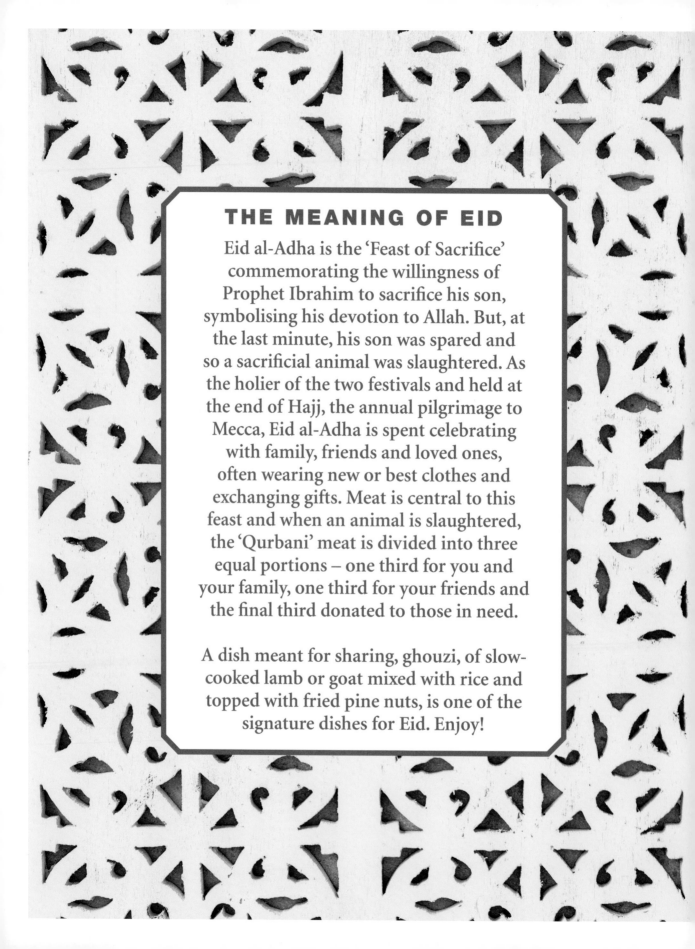

THE MEANING OF EID

Eid al-Adha is the 'Feast of Sacrifice' commemorating the willingness of Prophet Ibrahim to sacrifice his son, symbolising his devotion to Allah. But, at the last minute, his son was spared and so a sacrificial animal was slaughtered. As the holier of the two festivals and held at the end of Hajj, the annual pilgrimage to Mecca, Eid al-Adha is spent celebrating with family, friends and loved ones, often wearing new or best clothes and exchanging gifts. Meat is central to this feast and when an animal is slaughtered, the 'Qurbani' meat is divided into three equal portions – one third for you and your family, one third for your friends and the final third donated to those in need.

A dish meant for sharing, ghouzi, of slow-cooked lamb or goat mixed with rice and topped with fried pine nuts, is one of the signature dishes for Eid. Enjoy!

PRAWN BIRYANI

This is a truly celebratory recipe – luscious prawns bathed in a rich sauce then steamed in layers of fragrant basmati rice. The special touch is the rosewater and saffron, poured over the rice before it is steamed so it infuses everything with its delicate scent and anoints the top with golden orange strands.

Serves 4–6

400g/2 cups long basmati rice
1 tbsp olive oil
2 cinnamon sticks
4 whole cloves
2 bay leaves
4 cardamom pods

For the gravy
1 tbsp rosewater
a good pinch of saffron strands
3 red onions, finely sliced
2–3 tbsp cornflour
sunflower oil
2 red onions, diced
2 tbsp ghee
2 tsp coriander seeds
5 garlic cloves, crushed
5cm/2in piece fresh root ginger,
    finely grated
2 tbsp tomato purée
2 tsp garam masala
1 tsp turmeric
1 tsp mild curry powder
2 tsp ground cumin
3 medium tomatoes, diced
20g/½ cup coriander leaves,
    finely chopped
15g/½ cup mint, finely chopped
1kg/2/¼lb shelled prawns
150g/⅝ cup full-fat yogurt
juice of 1 lemon

Pour the rosewater into a bowl and add the saffron and 1 tablespoon of water. Set aside to infuse. Wash the rice well under cold running water, then tip into a bowl. Cover with plenty of cold water and soak for 20 minutes. Drain well.

In a bowl, mix the sliced red onions with 2 tablespoons cornflour until coated. Pour the sunflower oil into a pan to come up 5cm/2in of the side. Line a plate with kitchen paper. Heat the oil to 190°C/375°F or until a breadcrumb dropped into the hot oil sizzles furiously. Fry the coated onions in three or four batches until golden brown and crispy and draining as you go.

Bring a large pan of water to the boil and add the olive oil and the cinnamon sticks, cloves, bay leaves and cardamom pods. Add the rice, reduce the heat to low and cook for 5 minutes or until the grains of rice are half cooked. Strain and set aside. Keep the pan to use to cook the gravy. Heat 2 tablespoons sunflower oil in the saucepan. Stir in the diced red onions and sauté for 5–8 minutes until caramelised. Stir in the ghee and coriander seeds and sauté for around 1 minute until fragrant.

Add the garlic, ginger and tomato purée and cook for 1 minute. Sprinkle the garam masala, turmeric, curry powder, cumin and some black pepper on top and cook for 2 minutes. Season then add the tomatoes, half of the fried onions, the coriander and mint and cook, stirring, for 5–8 minutes or until a thick gravy forms. Stir in the prawns, the yogurt and lemon juice and cook over a low heat for a further 5 minutes. Take the pan off the heat.

In a wide casserole pan, pour in some sunflower oil until it just covers the bottom. Tilt the pan around so that it covers a little of the sides, too. Assemble the biryani, layering the ingredients in the pan, starting with a third of the rice, then half the gravy and prawns, then rice again and so on, finishing with rice.

Spoon the rosewater and saffron mix on top, along with the remaining fried onions. Place the pot over a low heat and cook for 30–40 minutes until the rice has completely cooked. Remove from the heat and serve.

KOFTAT SAMAK

These dense little fishcakes are often served as a starter. Instead of using breadcrumbs to coat the fish, the breadcrumbs are used in the mixture to slightly lighten the fishcake. You don't need to use an expensive piece of fish for this – anything with firm, white flesh is good here as it's combined with all the lovely spices.

Serves 4–6

For the fishcakes
1 medium onion, chopped
1 garlic clove, roughly chopped
375g/13oz firm, white fish,
    such as cod, haddock or
    halibut or Emperor fish in
    UAE, skinless and boneless
25g/½ cup fresh breadcrumbs
1 tsp ground coriander
1 tsp lime powder
½ tsp ground turmeric
½ tsp mild chilli powder
½ tsp ground black pepper
½ tsp salt
1 tbsp tomato purée
zest of 1 lemon
handful fresh coriander,
    torn, plus extra for garnish
vegetable oil for frying

For the tomato sauce
2 tbsp olive oil
1 small onion, finely chopped
1 garlic clove, crushed or grated
½ tsp ground coriander
½ tsp ground cumin
½ tsp mild chilli powder
2 tsp tomato purée
2 medium tomatoes, diced
juice of ½ lemon, plus extra
pinch of caster sugar

For the fishcakes, put the onion and garlic into a food processor and blitz until finely chopped. Add all the remaining ingredients (except the vegetable oil) for the fishcakes to the food processor and whizz together to form a rough paste. Scrape down the sides occasionally to make sure that everything is well chopped and incorporated.

Take a small handful of the mixture and gently squeeze together to form a small ball in the palm of your hand, then flatten to make a small cake approximately 5–6cm/2–2 ½in in diameter and 1cm/½in deep. Repeat to make 12 fishcakes in total. Cover and chill to allow them to firm up while you make the sauce.

Heat the olive oil in a medium-sized pan over a medium heat. Once hot, add the onion and fry for 4–5 minutes until softened.

Stir in the garlic, spices and tomato purée and fry for another 1–2 minutes.

Add the tomatoes, lemon juice and a couple of tablespoons of water. Season with salt and pepper. Stir together and simmer gently over a medium heat for 8–10 minutes, stirring occasionally, until the tomatoes are softened. Add a little more water if it's too dry.

Allow to cool a little before pouring into a mini processor, then blend until smooth to make a dipping sauce consistency. Add a pinch of sugar, taste and adjust the seasoning. Add a squeeze more lemon or water, to adjust the flavour and consistency if necessary.

To cook the fishcakes, heat 1cm/½in vegetable oil in a medium frying pan over a medium–high heat. When the oil is hot, fry the fishcakes in batches for 2½–3 minutes on each side until cooked through and no longer opaque in the centre. Remove with a slotted spatula and drain on kitchen paper.

Serve immediately with the tomato sauce for dipping.

PRAWNS IRSEYAH

This is a very simple dish to make and calls for just a handful of ingredients, but the ingredients transform it into a luxurious feast. It's finished with a couple of pan-fried prawns, a sprinkling of baby basil leaves and a couple of golden strands of saffron.

Serves 4–6

200g/1 cup basmati rice
300g/2 cups king prawns, peeled
2 tsp salt
20g ground cardamom
50g/3⅓ tbsp ghee, plus extra
   for frying
200g/scant 1 cup double cream
100g/⅔ cup parmesan cheese,
   grated
a pinch of saffron strands

To garnish
a few baby basil leaves and a
   pinch of saffron

Put the rice into a medium saucepan and add 600ml/2⅔ cups water. Swirl the pan around so that the rice sits in an even layer. Leave to soak for 1 hour.

Set aside a small handful of prawns for the garnish and add the remaining prawns and salt to the rice. Cover with a lid and bring to the boil. Reduce the heat to a simmer and cook for 10–12 minutes until the rice is cooked.

Add the cardamom, ghee, double cream, grated parmesan and saffron to the pan. Keeping it over a low heat, stir the mixture until it thickens slightly.

Take the pan off the heat and blend with a hand blender until smooth. Cover to keep warm.

Heat a knob of ghee in a frying pan and quickly pan fry the remaining prawns until they've turned completely pink and are cooked through.

Spoon the rice mixture onto a large warmed serving dish. Garnish with the cooked prawns, basil and saffron and serve.

MUHAMMAR RICE AND FRIED SAFI FISH

Being half Bahraini and half Emirati, I grew up with many mixed elements of both cultures and this is what I bring in this recipe. This dish is the one that everyone at home waits for the most at Eid al-Fitr because seafood is not widely consumed during the holy month of Ramadan. Also at Eid al-Adha, a lot of meat is offered because traditionally the sacrifices (cattle) would be cooked and eaten for lunch.

Serves 6–8

For the fish
4 tbsp sunflower or olive oil
5 garlic cloves, crushed or grated
juice of 1 large lemon
1 kg/2¼lb Safi fish or red mullet (around 12–18 small fish), cleaned, washed de-scaled and fins removed
250ml/generous 1 cup sunflower oil, for frying

For the spice mix
1 tsp freshly ground nutmeg
1 tbsp coriander powder
1 tbsp turmeric powder
1 tbsp cumin powder
½ tbsp mild curry powder
salt and freshly ground black pepper

For the rice
600g/3 cups long basmati rice
a pinch of saffron strands, lightly ground
1 tbsp rosewater
250ml/⅔ cups date molasses
2 tsp ground cinnamon
55g/½ stick salted butter, melted
3 cardamom pods, crushed
1 tbsp ground cardamom

Mix together all the ingredients for the spice mix and season with salt and pepper.

To prepare the fish, put the oil into a large bowl, stir in the garlic, lemon juice and spice mix and season. Add the fish. Rub the marinade into the fish, cover and set aside while you prepare the rice. Soak the rice with water for 30 minutes. In a separate bowl, soak the saffron in rosewater, set aside for at least 15 minutes.

Pour 1.5 litres/2½ pints water into a saucepan, stir in the date molasses and cinnamon and heat gently so that the molasses dissolves. Bring to a gentle simmer, add the rice and stir gently. Cover and reduce the heat. Let it cook for 8 minutes, then remove from the heat and drain. Don't overcook at this stage otherwise the spices will become bitter. As the rice cooks, start frying the fish. First line a large plate with kitchen paper. Next, pour the oil into a large deep frying pan and heat over a medium–high heat. Once hot, carefully lay the fish into the pan. The fish is very moist so take care as the oil may spit at this stage. Fry each fish for 3–4 minutes on each side until the skin is golden and the flesh is opaque. Use a slotted spoon or spatula to carefully lift the fish out of the pan and transfer to the kitchen paper to drain. Continue to cook the fish in batches until it's all done.

Finish the rice. Return the drained rice to the pan. Mix the melted butter, cardamom pods and ground cardamom together, then pour over the rice. Add the saffron-infused rosewater and stir to mix thoroughly. Cover tightly and cook over the lowest heat for 6–8 minutes. When the rice is ready, spoon it onto a large serving dish, removing the cardamom pods as you do so. Place the fish on a separate serving plate and serve alongside the rice. The fish can be placed on top of the rice in the same serving plate – it's just less of a mess if you serve them separately.

This meal is usually served with a side of spice-infused Arabic ghee, home-grown rocket leaves, sliced limes and sliced white onion and, of course, any homemade pickle of your choice.

SNACKS & DRINKS

Despite delicious meals, we still pick at a variety of treats. These could be homemade, gifts from friends and family or favourite goodies.

CORN AND CHILLI FRITTERS

These sweetcorn fritters are pan-fried with warming spices and fragrant fresh coriander. Team with a refreshing cucumber, mint and yogurt dip and serve these either as a snack or a nibble to hand round before the big festivities start.

Makes 10

340g/14oz can sweetcorn,
   drained
50g/½ cup chickpea flour
½ tsp baking powder
1 tsp chilli powder
½ tsp turmeric
3 tbsp freshly chopped coriander
1 medium egg, beaten
oil and butter, for shallow frying
salt and pepper

For the dip
½ cucumber
a good pinch of salt
250ml/1 cup natural yogurt
½ tsp dried mint

Start by making the dip. Coarsely grate the cucumber and place in a sieve. Sprinkle over the salt. Leave to drain over a bowl for 15 minutes.

Meanwhile, mix together the sweetcorn, chickpea flour, baking powder, chilli powder, turmeric, coriander and egg. Season well with salt and pepper. Set aside.

Using your hands, squeeze the excess water from the cucumber. Discard this liquid, then transfer the grated cucumber to a bowl. Stir in the yogurt and the dried mint. You won't need any salt as the cucumber will already be salty. Keep in the fridge until you're ready to serve.

Heat 1 tablespoon olive oil and a knob of butter in a frying pan over a medium heat. When the butter is foaming, using a dessertspoon, add spoonfuls of the sweetcorn batter into the pan. Cook them in batches, 4 or 5 at a time, so you don't overcrowd them. Allow to cook for 2–3 minutes so the underside browns, before flipping them over and cooking for a further 1–2 minutes.

Transfer to a plate and keep warm while you cook the remaining fritters, adding a little more oil and butter to the pan. Serve the warm fritters with the cucumber and yogurt dip.

FRESH FRUIT JUICES

Here are three refreshing drinks. The tart pomegranate is softened with a touch of honey, while the apple juice has a dash of health-giving turmeric, which produces a gorgeous golden hue. The last juice is a light and refreshing version of traditional lemonade, infused with a hint of mint.

All recipes serve 4

Pomegranate and ginger sparkler
4 large pomegranates
60g/1 cup fresh ginger, unpeeled and roughly chopped
runny honey, to taste
soda or sparkling water, to top up
plenty of ice

Put the pomegranate on a board and cut each into quarters. Carefully remove the thick peel from the outside of each. Load the pieces alternately with the ginger into a juicer and whizz to extract the juice.

Pour into a large jug and whisk in a little honey to taste. Pour among 4 glasses and top up with a splash of soda or sparkling water and a couple of ice cubes to serve.

Apple and turmeric booster
1.8kg/4lb apples, roughly chopped
½–1 tsp turmeric, to taste
plenty of ice

Load the apples into a juicer and blitz to extract the juice.

Scoop off as much of the scum as possible and discard, then whisk the ground turmeric into the juice.

Spoon 3–4 ice cubes in each of 4 glasses and pour in the juice. Serve straightaway.

Fresh lemonade with mint
2 large lemons, plus extra slices to garnish
100g/½ cup caster sugar
2 sprigs fresh mint, roughly chopped, plus extra to garnish
sparkling water
plenty of ice

Cut the lemons in half and squeeze the juice into a medium pan. Roughly chop the lemon shells and add to the pan with the sugar and 800ml/3½ cups water.

Heat gently to dissolve the sugar, then bring to the boil. Reduce the heat to a simmer and cook for around 8 minutes. Take the pan off the heat and add the mint to infuse. Set aside to cool.

As soon as the liquid has cooled, spoon 3–4 ice cubes into each of 4 glasses. Strain the liquid evenly among the glasses. Top up with sparkling water and garnish with extra lemon and mint before serving.

'On the morning of the celebration, it's traditional for the head of the family to take the children to the mosque for the Eid prayer. Afterwards, groups of people stand on the side of the road, wishing each other Eid Mubarak – happy holidays!'

DAHI BARRAS

These little dumplings dressed with yogurt are a cool, savoury snack usually eaten with tea during Ramadan for Iftar, the evening meal that ends the day's fast, during Eid festivals or even as a side to a main meal. The lentils are soaked overnight, then ground into a paste that's deep fried.

Serves 4

200g/scant 1 cup split black
    lentils (urad dal)
1 tsp salt, or to taste
2.5cm/1in piece fresh ginger,
    peeled and chopped
½ teaspoon chilli powder,
    or to taste
4 tbsp warm water
a pinch of baking powder
sunflower or vegetable oil,
    for deep-frying
1 tsp chilli flakes, to garnish

For the yogurt
735g/scant 3 cups full-fat
    natural yogurt
1 tsp caster sugar, or to taste
1½ teaspoon salt, or to taste

For the tempering
3 tbsp sunflower or vegetable oil
2 garlic cloves, peeled and sliced
4–5 dried red chillies
1 tsp whole cumin seeds
5–6 fresh curry leaves,
    or more to taste

Start the night before by soaking the lentils. First, rinse them well in a sieve, then put into a large bowl, cover with plenty of water and leave to soak overnight.

Drain and rinse the lentils. Put half into a food processor. Add the salt, ginger, chilli powder and 2 tablespoons warm water. Blend to make a thick paste. Transfer to a large bowl. Add the remaining lentils and baking powder to the processor with another 2 tablespoons warm water and blend. Add the rest of the mixture. Take an electric hand mixer and whisk for around 5 minutes.

Line a large tray or plate with kitchen paper. Pour enough oil into a wok or medium saucepan (or use a deep-fat fryer) to come up around a third of the way up the sides to deep-fry the dumplings. Heat the oil for 3–4 minutes until a cube of bread sizzles when dropped into the middle of the oil.

Take 2 teaspoons and, using one, scoop up some of the mixture. Use the other to gently nudge the mixture into the hot oil, then repeat four more times. The dumplings will bounce up to the top of the oil as they go into the pan. Fry for 3 minutes (1½ minutes each side) turning halfway through. Lift out with a slotted spoon and drain. Continue to shape and cook the mixture in batches.

Fill a large bowl with warm water and add the dumplings – they should be fully immersed in the water. Leave to soak for 10 minutes. Take each dumpling and gently press the water out with 4 fingers of one hand at the bottom of the dumpling and 4 fingers of the other hand at the top. Place the pressed dumplings in a serving dish.

Put the yogurt, sugar and salt into a bowl and mix until creamy. Spoon on top of the dumplings, giving the dish a little shake to evenly coat the pieces. Next, in a small frying pan, heat the oil for the tempering and then add the garlic, red chillies and cumin. Fry over a medium heat until golden brown, taking care not to let the pieces burn and blacken. Take the pan off the heat and add the curry leaves. Pour evenly on top of the yogurt. Sprinkle with chilli flakes and serve cold or at room temperature.

CHICKEN WITH MANGO CHUTNEY AND LIME

Crispy on the outside and juicy in the middle, this chicken makes great finger food for any celebration. The chicken is marinated first to add more flavour and you can do this up to one day before you cook it – the same goes for the mango dip. Just keep both stored in separate containers in the fridge.

Serves 4

1 tsp dried mint
1 tsp ground cumin
1 very small garlic clove,
    finely grated
finely grated zest and juice of
    1 lemon
1 tsp olive oil
2 x 150–175g/5–6oz skinless,
    boneless chicken breasts,
    cut into strips
about 1 litre/scant 4½ cups
    vegetable oil, for deep-frying
50g/½ cup plain flour
2 medium eggs
100g/1 cup dried breadcrumbs
sea salt flakes, for sprinkling

For the dip
200g/1⅔ cups mango chutney
good pinch of paprika
good pinch of ground cumin
finely grated zest ½ lime,
    plus 2 tsp lime juice

Start by marinating the chicken. Stir together the dried mint, cumin, garlic, zest and juice of the lemon as well as the olive oil. Add the chicken and mix well to ensure all the chicken strips are coated in the marinade. Set aside in the fridge for at least 1 hour and up to a day.

Meanwhile, mix together the ingredients for the dip. Set aside in a small serving bowl.

When you're ready to cook the chicken, pour the vegetable oil into a large pan. (It should only come halfway up the side of the pan). Heat over a medium heat to 180°C/350°F. To check the oil is hot enough, drop a cube of bread into the middle of the oil and it should sizzle and turn golden within a few seconds.

Tip the plain flour onto a plate. Beat the eggs with a splash of water in a shallow bowl and tip the breadcrumbs onto another plate. Remove the chicken from the marinade and pat dry with kitchen paper. Dip a chicken strip into the flour, shaking off any excess, then dip it into the egg mixture. Finally press into the breadcrumbs ensuring the piece is well coated. Continue with the remaining chicken strips.

As soon as the oil is at temperature, fry the chicken in batches for 4–5 minutes until golden golden, crispy and cooked through. Using tongs, transfer the chicken to a plate lined with kitchen paper to absorb extra oil. Transfer to a serving plate, sprinkle with sea salt flakes and serve with the mango dip. Best eaten straightaway.

SALTY LABAN

A basic laban is made with yogurt, water and salt. Here, a little mint has been added for freshness and then the mixture is whisked to create a frothy topping. The thickness of the yogurt you use can determine the thickness of the drink, so adjust with less or more water to produce the consistency you prefer.

Makes about 800ml 1½ pints, enough for 4 drinks

500g/2 cups natural yogurt, a natural set one is good
2 tbsp chopped fresh mint, plus extra for sprinkling, optional
2 good pinches of salt, or to taste
ice cubes

Put the yogurt and mint (if using) into a large bowl and pour in 200ml/1 cup water. Whisk with a stick blender or hand mixer until well mixed and frothy. Add salt to taste, adjust flavourings as needed, and whisk again.

Drop a few ice cubes into 4 tall glasses. Pour in the blended yogurt, then spoon the foam on top. Scatter over some finely chopped mint and serve immediately while still cold and frothy.

To make a sweet Laban
Omit the salt and blend in 1 tablespoon of clear honey instead.

To make a savoury Laban
Add 1 small grated or crushed garlic clove after adding the mint.

KHANFAROUSH

Khanfaroush is a sweet treat that is very typical of the Gulf region and often served on special occasions. They're made from storecupboard ingredients, flavoured with rosewater, cardamom and saffron and dusted with icing sugar to finish. Serve hot with coffee.

Makes 16

3 tbsp rice flour
1 tbsp plain flour
1 tbsp caster sugar
½ tsp baking powder
2 medium eggs
½–1 tbsp rosewater
seeds from 12 cardamom pods,
   crushed to a powder
a good pinch of saffron strands
1–2 tsp vegetable oil

To serve
icing sugar, to dust

Line a plate with kitchen paper.

Put both flours into a large bowl and add the sugar, baking powder, eggs, rosewater, cardamom powder and saffron. Mix well until smooth, then set the mixture aside for 30 minutes.

Heat around 1 teaspoon oil in a large frying pan over a medium heat. Once the oil has started to warm up, tilt the pan so that the oil covers the base.

Use a teaspoon or half-tablespoon measure to drop spoonfuls of the batter into the pan, around 4–5 at a time, and fry them on both sides until they're golden brown.

Lift onto the lined plate to absorb any excess oil.

Dust with icing sugar and serve straightaway.

DATES BETHETHA

The combination in this recipe of dates, rich in fibre and minerals that give you energy, and spices which offer an aromatic fresh taste, is very special. Another added bonus is that it can be kept fresh for longer compared to other desserts – you can make it up to three days ahead. Store in the fridge and take out around one hour before serving.

Serves 4–6

115g/1 cup wholemeal flour
1 tsp ground cardamom
1 tsp ground ginger
1 tsp ground star anise
200g/generous 1 cup ready-to-
    eat soft seedless dates, finely
    chopped
50g/3⅓ tbsp ghee, melted

To serve
finely chopped walnuts
    or almonds

Tip the flour into a large frying pan and place over a medium heat. Cook for 2–3 minutes, stirring constantly, until the flour turns golden brown and smells nutty. Rest a sieve on a large bowl and tip the flour into the sieve. Add the spices and sift both to mix together.

Toss the dates in the flour, then with your fingers, rub the dates into the flour, squeezing the fruit constantly to break it down. Continue to do this until the mixture looks like a crumble.

Slowly pour the ghee into the bowl and mix together. Keep rubbing the flour and dates together until all the ingredients are incorporated.

Divide the mixture among 4 or 6 small serving bowls, scatter over the nuts and serve with a cup of coffee.

BANANA, MANGO AND PAPAYA SMOOTHIE

This is a refreshing snack, dotted with chunks of fresh mango and toasted coconut flakes. If you've never tried fresh turmeric before, add a little to start with, so that you can check you like the overall taste. This smoothie stores well in the fridge – just give it a whisk before serving in case the mixture has started to separate slightly.

Serves 4

1 medium, ripe mango,
    stoned and chopped
2 ripe papayas, halved,
    deseeded and chopped
1 medium banana, chopped
120ml/½ cup coconut milk
1.5cm/ ¾in piece fresh
    turmeric, grated
2 pinches each of freshly
    ground black pepper and
    cinnamon
juice of 1 lime

To garnish
coconut flakes, toasted if liked

Set aside a couple of spoonfuls of chopped mango and put the rest into a blender.

Add the papaya, banana, coconut milk, fresh turmeric, spices and lime juice. Pour in 120ml/½ cup cold water and blend until smooth.

Divide the smoothie among 4 glasses and top with the reserved mango and the coconut flakes.

Cook's tip
If you have coconut milk left over that you're not going to use straightaway, pour into a sealable container and freeze for up to one month.

'Ahead of Eid, families prepare for the celebration by purchasing new clothes for their children. The markets are lit up and crowded, and shopping continues until dawn.'

MINI SPICED DATE LOAVES

These little loaves, flavoured with dates and warm spices, make a delicious dessert or treat for afternoon tea. They're easy to make, as the method is based on a traditional cake mix, but the batter is slightly wetter which creates a light and soft texture. They're delicious on their own but even more special with a cream-cheese frosting.

Makes 12

130g/¾ cup pitted dates, chopped
1 tsp bicarbonate of soda
200g/2 cups plain flour
¼ tsp ground ginger
¼ tsp ground cinnamon
½ tsp ground cardamom
½ tsp salt
115g/1¼ sticks unsalted butter, at room temperature, chopped, plus extra to grease
175g/generous ⅔ cups caster sugar
2 eggs, at room temperature
1 tsp vanilla extract

For the frosting
150g/1½ sticks unsalted butter, room temperature, chopped
200g/1⅔ cups icing sugar, sifted
200g/scant 1 cup cream cheese, at room temperature

To decorate
dried rose petals, slithered pistachios and perhaps a little touch of gold dust

Preheat the oven to 180°C fan/400°F/gas mark 6. Grease a 12-hole loaf-shaped tin, then line each hole with baking parchment. Set aside.

Put the dates in a medium bowl and pour 300ml/1⅓ cups boiling water over them. Leave to soften for 2 minutes, then stir in the bicarbonate of soda and set aside.

In another bowl, sift the flour, ground ginger, cinnamon, cardamom and salt and set aside.

Cream the butter and sugar together in a bowl until light and fluffy. Add the eggs, one at a time, making sure to scrape the sides after each addition. Whisk in the vanilla extract to combine. Add in the flour mix, alternating with the date mix, starting and ending with the flour. Beat until the batter is fully combined. This is quite a runny mix but it gives a lovely rise to the finished cakes and makes them really moist, too.

Pour or spoon the batter into the lined tins and bake for 20–25 minutes or until a skewer inserted into the loaves comes out clean. Remove from the oven and set aside for 2 minutes to cool slightly in the tin. Lift onto a wire rack to cool completely.

For the frosting, cream the butter and icing sugar together in a bowl until light and fluffy. Add the cream cheese and fold in carefully to combine everything together.

Transfer the frosting to a piping bag fitted with a star nozzle and chill until it is firm enough to pipe.

As soon as the loaves are completely cool, decorate them with the frosting and garnish as desired.

KARAK TEA

This is a rich, sweet-tasting tea, best made fresh and served straightaway. All the ingredients are simmered together so the spices and ginger infuse the drink with lots of lovely flavours. Serve in small glasses, garnished with a strand of golden saffron. Pair with Rangina (see page 164 for recipe).

Serves 6

For the tea
½ tsp ground ginger
25g/1oz granulated or
  caster sugar
1 slightly heaped tsp
  ground cardamom
12g/¼ cup fresh root ginger,
  sliced
2 tbsp black loose-leaf tea
65ml/¼ cup condensed milk
225ml/scant 1 cup evaporated
  milk
a pinch of saffron
200ml/scant 1 cup whole milk
500ml/generous 2 cups water

To serve
6 strands of saffron

Put all the ingredients for the tea into a large saucepan. Bring to the boil and as soon as the liquid is boiling, turn the heat down to a low simmer.

Simmer for 20–25 minutes, but watch the pan carefully because if the mixture gets too hot it can boil over.

Serve the tea in 6 small glasses, each garnished with a saffron strand.

DESSERTS

Each dessert is a treat in itself. Many
are dishes that you only have on Eid
each year and so you look forward to
them with huge anticipation.

KHANFAROOSH

These saffron and cardamom mini cakes are a tradition in themselves and feature at every Eid gathering. The original recipe deep-fries the batter, whereas this version bakes the mix. Be generous when sprinkling the sesame seeds into the tins as the nuttiness complements the sweetness. A freshly baked batch smells like Eid!

Makes 24

a pinch of saffron (or as
   generous as you feel)
2 tbsp rosewater
60ml/4 tbsp vegetable oil, plus
   extra for brushing
30g/¼ cup sesame seeds (toast
   them for an intense flavour)
3 large eggs
175g/generous ¾ cup caster
   sugar
1 tsp vanilla extract
60ml/4 tbsp whole milk
125g/1 generous cup plain flour
80g/¾ cup semolina (or sifted
   rice flour)
2 tsp baking powder
1 tbsp finely ground cardamom

Preheat the oven to 170°C fan/375°F/gas mark 5. Put the saffron and rosewater in a small bowl and leave to infuse for at least 15 minutes.

Use a little vegetable oil to brush the inside of two 12-hole muffin tins and generously sprinkle the sesame seeds inside each mould. If you don't have 2 muffin tins, bake the cakes in two batches.

Mix the eggs and sugar together using an electric hand whisk (or in a freestanding mixer) until thick, light and creamy. This will take about 3 minutes. Then add the vanilla extract, vegetable oil and the milk. Beat briefly until well combined. The mixture should be like a soft batter.

Combine the flour, semolina, baking powder and cardamom in a bowl and add around a third of this mixture to eggs and sugar mix. Fold in with a large metal spoon, then do the same again in two more stages.

Carefully pour in the saffron-infused rosewater and fold in, again using the metal spoon, until the mixture is smooth. Take care when pouring it in: if it splashes on anything, it's tattooed!

Use a metal tablespoon to spoon the mixture evenly among the prepared muffin tin holes. Bake for 10–15 minutes until golden and firm to the touch.

Carefully loosen the edges and sides of each khanfaroosh with a small palette knife, then remove them from the tins and place on a wire rack to cool. They're particularly delicious when they're just warm.

CHAMMI DATES

These dates are stuffed with a homemade cheese, which sounds like an odd combination but really does work. The cheese is actually really simple and calls for just two ingredients – milk and lemon – which are simmered together to make a curd and then sweetened to balance the flavour of the dates.

Makes 15

500ml/generous 2 cups
    full-fat milk
1½ tsp lemon juice
1 tbsp caster sugar
15 whole dates
60g/2½oz white chocolate,
    melted
30g/¼ cup pistachios, finely
    chopped

Pour the milk into a medium, heavy-based saucepan and bring to the boil.

Add the lemon juice, then reduce the heat to low–medium and simmer for about 20 minutes so that the milk curdles. The liquid will evaporate slightly and separate so that curds form on top.

Line a sieve with muslin (or use a clean J-cloth) and rest it over a bowl. Pour the milk and curds into the sieve. Let the milk drain into the bowl and, when most of it has gone, gently press the curds with the back of a spoon to extract as much liquid as possible. The remaining curds will be soft.

Tip the drained curds into a bowl. Stir in the sugar and mix well until thoroughly combined, then transfer the bowl to the fridge to chill. This is what's called 'chammi'. If you want to prepare in advance, make the chammi up to 1–2 days before and store it in a sealed container in the fridge.

Use a small sharp knife to make a slit lengthways along each date. Prise the dates apart and remove the long thin seeds. Use a teaspoon to fill each date with chammi. Dip one end of each date into the melted white chocolate, then coat it with the pistachio nuts. Allow to cool until set. (If making ahead, keep the stuffed dates in the fridge.)

Arrange on a plate and serve.

LGEIMAT

These sweet, deep-fried dumplings, drizzled with date molasses just before serving, are a popular Emirati favourite for Iftar during Ramadan. They're like many of our traditional recipes – inherited from our grandmothers then passed down through the generations and loved by families to come.

Serves 6 (makes around 30)

280g/2½ cups flour
125g/generous 1 cup milk
   powder
2 x 7g/¼oz sachets instant yeast
1 tsp baking powder
1 tsp ground cardamom
1 tsp sugar
1 egg
1 tbsp sunflower or vegetable
   oil, plus extra for deep-frying

To serve
date molasses or syrup

Put the flour into a large bowl. Add the milk powder, yeast, baking powder, cardamom and sugar and mix well.

Whisk the egg, 1 tablespoon of oil and 225ml/1 cup cold water together in a separate bowl or jug. Make a well in the centre of the dry ingredients and pour the wet mix into the bowl, stirring vigorously to incorporate. Cover and set aside for 1 hour so that the yeast and baking powder activate.

Heat the oil in a deep-fat fryer or large deep pan to 180°C/350°F or until a cube of bread sizzles when dropped into it. Line a large tray with kitchen paper.

Using 2 teaspoons, scoop up some of the mixture with one and use the other to carefully drop the mixture into the hot oil. Fry for 4–5 minutes until golden brown and cooked through in the centre. Repeat, cooking in batches of 4 or 5. Lift out with a slotted spoon as soon as each batch is done and drain on the kitchen paper.

To serve, scoop into bowls and drizzle with date molasses.

KHABEESA TRIFLE

There's a good contrast here in terms of flavour and texture between the crumbly khabeesa and the vanilla-scented cream. A string of redcurrants on top provides a pop of colour and just enough refreshing acidity to cut through the richness of it all. Any leftovers of either layer can be stored in the fridge for up to five days.

Serves 6–8

For the khabeesa
350g/generous 3 cups
   plain flour
a pinch of saffron strands,
   lightly ground
225g/1 cup caster sugar
2 tsp–1 tbsp rosewater
a pinch of ground turmeric
a pinch of ground cardamom
½ pinch salt
225g/1 cup ghee
30g/⅓ cup slivered or chopped
   pistachios, chopped
100g/scant 1 cup ground
   almonds
30g/¼ cup flaked almonds

For the vanilla cream
325g/1½ cups mascarpone
   cheese
100g/⅖ cup whipping cream
75g/⅓ cup full-fat milk
1½ tsp vanilla extract
30g/1¼oz caster sugar

To decorate
fresh redcurrants, chopped
   pistachios and icing sugar,
   to dust

Pour the flour into a large heavy-based pan and toast over a medium heat until it turns golden brown – this will take about 10 minutes. Be careful not to burn the flour – keep stirring until the raw flavour has disappeared.

In another pan, pour in 500ml/generous 2 cups water and add the saffron and sugar. Bring to a boil and stir well so that the saffron steeps in the liquid to infuse it.

Gradually pour the water into the flour, whisking continuously. Pour in the rosewater, turmeric and ground cardamom and salt and mix well.

Add the ghee, pistachios, ground and flaked almonds, stirring well until the mixture is crumbly. Tip onto a large tray and spread out to cool.

To make the vanilla cream, put the mascarpone into a bowl and use a wooden spoon to soften it. Add the whipping cream, milk, vanilla extract and sugar and, using an electric hand whisk on a low setting, carefully combine all the ingredients together. Don't overwhisk.

Spoon into a piping bag, seal the end and transfer to the fridge to cool.

Take 6 glass serving dishes – ice-cream sundae dishes are handy here – and spoon and pipe the khabeesa and vanilla cream alternately, to create contrasting layers.

To finish, spoon a dollop of the cream on top and garnish with strings of redcurrants, pistachios and a little icing sugar.

‘Eid reminds me of when my mum would make huge pastries and I'd demolish two or three in one sitting!’

See recipe overleaf

LEMON-ROSE EID CAKE

This is a beautiful celebratory cake, perfect for this special occasion. Both the cake and the icing have a fresh lemony taste and there's a hint of spice, too. Making the sponges two or three days ahead helps the flavours to come together – once baked, leave them to cool completely, wrap in clingfilm and store in an airtight container.

Cuts into about 14–16 slices

For the cake
30g/¼ cup ground almonds
225g/2¼ sticks unsalted butter,
    at room temperature,
    cut into cubes
225g/1 cup caster sugar
215g /2 cups self-raising flour
2 tsp baking powder
4 large eggs
½ tsp vanilla extract
½ tsp ground cinnamon
1 tsp ground cardamom
    (or ground cardamom seeds)
finely grated zest 1 lemon

**For the white chocolate
buttercream icing**
200g/7oz white chocolate,
    chopped into small pieces
500g/4 cups icing sugar
225g/2¼ sticks unsalted butter,
    at room temperature,
    cut into cubes
½ tsp vanilla extract
2 tbsp strained lemon juice

Preheat the oven to 160°C fan/350°F/gas mark 4. Lightly butter two 20cm x 4cm/8 x 1½in deep, loose-bottomed cake tins and line the bases with baking paper.

Heat a small, heavy-based frying pan over a medium heat, add the ground almonds and toast in the dry pan, stirring occasionally until pale golden, about 3–5 minutes. Tip onto a plate to cool.

Put the butter, caster sugar, flour, toasted ground almonds, baking powder, eggs, vanilla, cinnamon and cardamom in a large bowl and whisk with an electric hand whisk for 2 minutes until smooth. Fold in the lemon zest. Divide the mixture evenly between the 2 cake tins and gently level the tops. Bake for about 25 minutes until the tops feel firm and the sides of the cake start to shrink away from the sides of the tin. Remove from the oven, loosen the sides with a small palette knife and leave for a few minutes before turning out onto a wire rack. Peel off the lining paper and leave the cakes to cool completely.

Meanwhile, make the white chocolate buttercream. Melt the chocolate in the microwave or in a bowl set over a pan of very gently simmering water, making sure the base doesn't touch the water. When the chocolate has started to melt, remove the bowl and the pan from the heat (so it doesn't overheat) and let the chocolate finish melting, stirring occasionally. Once melted, remove the bowl from the pan and leave the chocolate to cool but so it still remains runny.

Sift the icing sugar into a large bowl, add the butter and beat together with an electric hand whisk (on low speed to begin with) until softened, smooth and well mixed. Beat in the melted chocolate with a wooden spoon, then the vanilla and lemon juice.

For the decoration
dried rose petals
pink, white and yellow
  sugared almonds
icing sugar for dusting
gold dust and gold leaf, optional

When the cakes are cold, carefully slice each one in half (see tip below). Lay the base of one of the halves on a flat serving plate. Save the base layer of the other cake for the top of the cake. Using about half of the buttercream for the layering, spread the first cake layer with some of the buttercream. Lay another piece of cake on top. Continue the spreading and layering to build up the cake into 4 layers, putting the saved base of the final piece of cake on top, to give a flat top.

Brush any loose crumbs off the outside of the cake. Carefully spread the remaining buttercream over the top and sides of the cake. Smooth the surface with a wide spatula or palette knife.

Decorate with rose petals and sugared almonds and finish with gold dust and gold leaf, if using. Dust with icing sugar (see photo).

Cook's tip
So the cakes layers are of even widths when you cut them, first go all round the middle of the side of each cake with a long serrated knife, cutting into it slightly, to mark out the centre. When you then slice through each cake to halve it, you can follow this mark with your knife as a guide for halving it equally.

If either of the cakes bake unevenly on top, shave a little off to level them.

ASEEDA BOBAR

Aseeda, a sweet pumpkin pudding, is a very old Emirati dessert. It is one of our most famous sweet dishes. It may sound strange to use pumpkin or squash in a dessert, but it works perfectly thanks to its natural sweetness. Flour, ghee and a little added sugar combine with the purée, then rosewater, saffron and cardomom are stirred in.

Serves 4

100g/1 cup plain flour
2 tbsp currants, to decorate
300g/2 cups pumpkin or
   butternut squash, chopped
   into 2cm/¾in cubes
15g/1 tbsp ghee
80g/⅓ cup caster sugar
2 tsp rosewater
a good pinch of saffron
½ tsp ground cardamom

Preheat the oven to 180°C fan/400°F/gas mark 6.

Spread the flour evenly on a baking tray. Roast the flour in the middle of the oven for about 20 minutes until it turns golden, stirring it halfway through so that it colours evenly.

Put the currants into a small bowl and cover with warm water. Set aside to plump up.

Put the pumpkin or squash in a medium saucepan and cover with cold water. Bring to the boil, then reduce the heat and simmer until it's very soft – about 25–30 minutes. Strain the cooking water into a bowl and reserve, then return the squash to the saucepan and mash until smooth.

Add in the ghee, sugar, rosewater, saffron, cardamom and the roasted flour and mix well.

Over a very low heat and stirring constantly, cook for around 2 minutes. If the mixture seems very thick and needs softening, beat in 2–3 tablespoons of the reserved pumpkin cooking water.

Divide the mixture among 4 small serving bowls. Drain the currants, then spoon over the mixture to garnish.

SAGO PUDDING

Sago is similar to rice, except that it is round and holds its texture once cooked. It's made from the pith of tropical palm trees and needs to be soaked before cooking. Here, it has to chill too, after it's been cooked, so forward planning is needed if you want to make this. Once made, the basic mixture will keep in the fridge for a couple of days.

Serves 6, generously

120g/¾ cup sago
100g/½ cup caster sugar, plus a
    little extra, to taste
500ml/generous 2 cups
    whole milk
1 tbsp rosewater
100g/1 cup pistachios, finely
    chopped
vanilla ice cream,
    slightly softened
dried rose petals, optional

In a mixing bowl, mix together the sago and 480ml/generous 2 cups water. Cover and leave to soak overnight. As it soaks, the sago will absorb some of the water and expand.

The next day, drain the sago through a sieve.

In a heavy saucepan, pour in 450ml/2 cups water, then add the sugar. Place the pan over a medium heat and stir to dissolve the sugar. Bring to the boil.

Add the soaked sago to the water and continue to stir as the mixture comes back to the boil. Lower the heat and cook, stirring, for about 20–25 minutes until the mixture has thickened, looks glossy and the sago has become transparent.

Once the mixture has reduced and thickened and drops thickly from the spoon like a soft jam, pour in the milk and rosewater. Bring to the boil, then lower the heat and simmer gently for 20 minutes. Stir very often as the mixture can stick on the bottom of the pan and turn brown.

Taste the sago and check it's sweet enough, adding more sugar if necessary, and see whether it needs a touch more rosewater. Once it's reduced and is a bit thicker, stir in 80g/¾ cup of the pistachios.

Pour the pudding mixture into a large bowl or container and allow to cool completely. Cover the top with baking parchment to prevent a skin forming, then chill in the fridge for several hours or overnight. The pudding will thicken again as it chills.

For each person, scoop out 2 heaped tablespoonfuls of the chilled pudding into a bowl, add 1–2 scoops of ice cream, mix well and transfer to a serving dish. Repeat this for each serving.

Sprinkle each pudding with the remaining pistachios and a few rose petals, if you wish. Serve cold.

HALWAT AL TAMUR BIL RUTAB

This is usually made with pitted khalas dates, but when rutab dates are in season they're perfect to use. This dessert is very simple and is a reminder of the way mothers and grandmothers used to cook in the past. Once made, this can be kept for a couple of days in the fridge. Simply reheat in the microwave and serve.

Serves 6

2 heaped tbsp of ghee
105g/1 cup wholewheat flour
500g/2⅞ cups pitted fresh
   rutab dates (not khunaizi),
   chopped
½ tbsp ground fennel
½ tbsp ground cardamom

To serve
yogurt and slivered pistachios

Put the ghee into a medium pan and melt over a medium heat. Stir in the flour.

Keep stirring until the flour is browned, about 5–7 minutes – but don't cook for too long or the flour will burn.

Add the dates. Remove the pan from the heat and stir well. Add the fennel and cardamom and stir until everything is combined. The dates should blend into the flour mixture.

Spoon into a bowl and serve with the yogurt and pistachios.

QURS

This Emirati dessert calls for just a handful of ingredients. The dough is rolled into rounds, cooked in a pan to make flatbreads, then tossed in sugar and melted ghee. It is often made in winter and used to be cooked on the fire.

Serves 4–6

150g/1½ cups plain wholemeal flour, plus extra for dusting
1 tsp salt
6 dates, pitted and chopped
125ml/generous 1 cup warm water
100g/1 stick ghee or butter, melted
170g/¾ cup caster sugar

Mix the flour and salt together in a large bowl.

In a separate bowl, mix the dates with the warm water. Leave to soften for 5–10 minutes.

Add the water and the soaked dates to the flour and mix to make a soft dough. Knead lightly until it comes together.

Divide the dough into 6 balls.

Dust a clean work surface or board with some of the flour. Using a rolling pin, roll each ball into a round, approximately 10cm/4in in diameter.

Heat a large frying pan over a high heat. When hot, dry-fry each round of flattened dough in the pan for 2–3 minutes on each side, until slightly puffed up and browned all over.

While the breads are still warm, tear them into small pieces and mix them in a bowl with the melted ghee and sugar until evenly coated.

Spoon onto a plate and serve.

RANGINA

These delicious little sweet date squares combine wholemeal flour, butter, sugar and cardamom to make a biscuit base that is topped with sweet dried fruit and mixed nuts. It's gorgeous on its own and even better with a small spoonful of creamy rich yogurt on the side and a cup of strong Arabic coffee.

Makes 16 squares

210g/2 cups wholemeal flour
100g/½ cup caster sugar
½ tbsp ground cardamom
135g/1¼ sticks unsalted butter, melted, plus extra for brushing
180g/1 cup ready-to-eat (i.e. soft) pitted dates, roughly chopped
60g/½ cup walnuts, chopped
30g/¼ cup pistachios, finely chopped

Use a little melted butter to brush an 18 x 18cm/7 x 7in square tin, then line with baking parchment.

Put the flour into a medium pan and cook over a medium–high heat, stirring occasionally, until slightly browned. This will take around 10 minutes. Remove the pan from the heat and set aside to cool.

Add the sugar, cardamom and melted butter and stir everything together well to make a mixture that's slightly crumbly. Take care not to stir it so much that it becomes dough-like. Spoon into the lined tin and press the mixture into the base evenly, using the back of a spoon to flatten it out.

Put the dates into a microwaveable bowl and place in the microwave. Cook for about 30 seconds to soften. If you don't have a microwave, put them into a pan and add 1–2 tablespoons water. Cover and cook over a very low heat, for around 5 minutes. Squish down with a spoon to check they've softened. Set aside to cool.

Once cooled, tip the dates into the tin and press into the mixture, again smoothing them evenly over the base.

Sprinkle the walnuts and pistachios over the top and press the nuts slightly into the dates so they stick. Transfer the tray to the fridge for about 2–3 hours or overnight if possible.

When ready to serve, lift out the baking paper and put on a board. Cut the rangina into squares.

Serve with yogurt and Arabic coffee or karak tea (see page 138).

PISTACHIO, CRANBERRY AND COCONUT BURFI

These moreish sweets are studded with cranberries and pistachios and flavoured with coconut and cardamom. They're particularly good with a strong black coffee or mint tea. Any leftovers can be stored in an airtight container for 4–5 days.

Makes 42 pieces

400g/1¾ cups caster sugar
500g/4½ cups milk powder
200ml/1 cup double cream
175g/generous 1 cup
  dried cranberries
60g/½ cup pistachios, finely
  chopped
70g/¾ cup desiccated coconut
1 tsp ground cardamom
155g/1½ stick unsalted butter,
  chopped, plus extra for
  greasing

Grease a 20 x 20cm/8 x 8in plastic container and set aside.

Pour the sugar into a large saucepan and add 120ml/½ cup water. Place over a low heat and stir with a metal spoon until the sugar has completely dissolved.

While the sugar syrup is heating, mix the milk powder and cream together in a large bowl until they are combined and have a breadcrumb consistency. Add the cranberries, pistachios, coconut and cardamom and mix loosely with a fork.

Once the sugar has dissolved, add the chopped butter to the pan and stir in. Once the butter has melted and the mixture comes to the boil, let it bubble for about 8 minutes or until the syrup is sticky. The longer you boil the syrup for, the harder the texture of the burfi will be.

Add the dried milk mixture to the pan and stir well until everything is combined. Tip into the greased container and level with the back of a spoon. Set aside to cool and set.

Tip out onto a board, slice into small squares and serve.

APPLE AND SULTANA FILO PARCELS

These simple baked parcels are easy to make and there's no need for any special equipment so this is a great recipe for the whole family to help with. Cook the apples until they're still just holding their shape so they will retain a little texture when baked.

Makes 8

4 Granny Smith apples
   (about 500g/18oz), peeled
   and chopped
6 cardamom pods,
   seeds crushed
½ tsp ground cinnamon
2 tbsp clear honey
1 tbsp sultanas
2 tbsp lemon juice
250g/9oz packet ready-made
   filo pastry
100g/1 stick unsalted butter,
   melted
2 tsp caster sugar
½ tsp ground cinnamon

Put the apples into a pan with the cardamom, cinnamon, honey, sultanas and lemon juice. Cover and simmer for 5–8 minutes until the apples are just soft, but still holding their shape. Leave to cool.

Preheat the oven to 180°C fan/400°F/gas mark 6.

Cut 24 pieces of pastry, three per parcel, each measuring 10 x 13cm/4 x 5¼in. Brush one piece lightly with melted butter. Place another piece on top. Brush again with butter and place the third piece on top.

Place a heaped tablespoon of the apple mixture on one end of the pastry. Take the right corner and fold diagonally to the left, enclosing the filling in a triangle shape. Fold this covered triangle up horizontally to enclose the triangle completely in filo. You'll now have a triangle at the end of the pastry. Now fold the triangle to the right to cover again and continue to fold up and to the left and right and so on until all the pastry is wrapped around the filling and has been used up. Do the same again with the other pieces until you have made 8 parcels.

Place on a baking sheet and brush lightly with melted butter. To finish, mix together the sugar and cinnamon and sprinkle over the parcels. Bake for about 15 minutes until crisp and golden.

GHURAIBA BISCUITS

These small, melt-in-the-mouth biscuits made with buttery ghee, sweetened with icing sugar and scented with ground cardamom are a delight. The finishing touch – a blanched almond half – is nudged into the middle of the rounds of dough just before going into the oven so they set there as they bake.

Makes about 18

155g/1½ cups plain or wholemeal flour

35g/¼ cup icing sugar, sifted

½ tsp ground cardamom

¼ rounded tsp baking powder

95g/½ cup chilled ghee – use cold from the fridge

about 9 whole, blanched almonds, split in half for decoration

Preheat the oven to 160°C fan/350°F/gas mark 4.

Put the flour into a medium bowl. Add the icing sugar, cardamom and baking powder. Stir everything together to mix well.

Use a spoon to scoop small pieces of ghee into the mixture then start mixing the mixture with your hands, rubbing the ghee into the flour, until all the ingredients come together into a dough. Shape it into a ball with your hands.

To shape each biscuit, take a small piece of the dough (about the size of a small walnut) and form into a ball. Place onto a baking tray (no need for parchment paper), then continue to make more balls with the rest of the dough, spacing the biscuits slightly apart.

When you've used up all the dough, lightly press half an almond onto each piece.

Bake for 12–14 minutes until they're slightly golden on the bottom but still pale on top. The almonds will be tinged very slightly brown, too.

Transfer to a wire rack to cool. Store in an airtight container for up to 1 week.

'Eid is all about food and sharing. In our house,
it is tradition to share plates of sweet treats
amongst the neighbours, Muslim or otherwise,
so that they can celebrate Eid with us.'

See recipes overleaf

CARDAMOM SCONES & EVERYTHING NICE

This recipe makes delicately scented scones that rise well. Instead of cream and jam, try making your own cream cheese, which is very easy, and a sweet pumpkin caramel spread. Both can be made ahead if you need to.

Makes 8 scones

For the scones

250g/2¼ cups self-raising flour, plus extra for dusting

1 tsp baking powder

1 tbsp caster sugar

1 tsp ground cardamom

½ vanilla pod

75g/¾ stick cold unsalted butter, cubed, plus extra to grease

75ml/⅓ cup cold milk, plus extra if needed

1 medium egg

To glaze

extra virgin olive oil or half olive oil/half milk or egg wash (1 egg beaten together with 1 tsp of water or milk)

Preheat the oven to 180°C fan/400°F/gas mark 6. Grease a baking sheet, then lightly dust with flour.

Combine all the dry ingredients in a medium-sized bowl and stir together well.

Slice the vanilla pod lengthways, then use the tip of a small knife to open up the pod and scrape the seeds. Add to the mix and stir in.

Using your fingers, rub the cubes of butter into the flour until it resembles breadcrumbs. Add the milk and egg and stir together with a round-bladed table knife to make a soft dough. Don't overwork the mixture though, clumps are fine! If it's not coming together, add a splash more milk.

When the dough comes together, roughly form it into a ball and wrap in baking parchment. Transfer to the fridge to chill for 10–15 minutes.

Roll out on a lightly floured surface until it's around 2cm/¾in thick.

Using a 6cm/2½in floured cutter, stamp out 3–4 scones and place them flat-side down on the prepared baking sheet. Push down with the cutter – don't be tempted to twist as this can result in a wonky scone. Gently knead back the off-cuts and cut out more scones. You should end up with 8 scones.

Brush the tops with one of the glazes and bake for 15 minutes until well risen and golden. Eat them hot or let them cool – it's up to you, depending on how patient you can be! Serve with the cream cheese and salted pumpkin caramel.

For the cream cheese

This makes a smooth, light cream cheese and works particularly well to offset the sweetness of the caramel. Beat a handful of chopped herbs into any leftovers for a quick dip or spread for flatbreads.

1 litre/1¾ pints full-fat milk
juice of 1 lemon
3 tbsp lime juice (around 1 large juicy lime)
a pinch of salt – add more if you like it salty

Line a sieve with muslin or cheesecloth and rest over a bowl.

In a medium saucepan, bring the milk to a simmer over a medium–high heat. Pour in the lemon juice and the lime juice slowly, while stirring continuously. Reduce the heat to medium and continue stirring. Watch it carefully as the mixture can curdle at any moment.

As soon as a greenish clear liquid forms and the cheese curds float on top, remove the pan from the heat and strain the mixture through the lined sieve. Let it sit in the sieve until it cools.

Lift the strained cheese curds into the bowl of a food processor and add a pinch of salt. Blend well until the consistency is smooth. Don't over process the mixture or it will turn into butter!

Scrape the mixture into a small wide-necked jar or container and store in the fridge for up to 1 week.

For the salted pumpkin caramel

To cook the pumpkin or squash, put it in a pan and part cover with water. Cover and bring to the boil. Reduce the heat and simmer until soft, about 15–20 minutes.

85g/⅔ cup light soft brown sugar
25g/¼ stick unsalted butter
250g/1⅔ cups cooked pumpkin or butternut squash, diced
4 tbsp double cream
1 tsp ground cinnamon powder
2 grates of fresh nutmeg
a pinch of sea salt
25–50g/¼– ½ cup pecans, chopped, to taste

Put the sugar and butter into a small saucepan over a high heat. Stir together as the butter melts to dissolve the sugar. Stir in the pumpkin.

Add the double cream and spices and stir continually to make a caramel consistency. Stir in the salt and chopped pecans.

Take the pan off the heat and let it cool, then spoon the mixture into a small jar or container.

Serve with the scones and cream cheese. Any leftover caramel can be stored at room temperature for up to 5 days.

BATHITHA TRUFFLES

Delicately scented with fennel with no added sugar, these are made by pulsing dates with flour. Take care when toasting the flour in the pan – too high a heat will burn the flour. You can make the balls the day before and then decorate. This also allows the flavour of the spice to develop and infuse the truffles. They'll keep for up to five days.

Makes 20

200g/2 cups plain flour
180g/1⅛ cup pitted dates, roughly chopped
1 heaped tsp ground cardamom
20g/¾oz finely ground fennel seeds
100g/½ cup ghee

To garnish
80–100g/3¼–3½oz white chocolate, melted
50g/½ cup pistachios, finely chopped

Line a board, baking sheet or cooling rack with baking parchment.

Place a large non-stick frying pan over a medium heat and tip in the flour. Toast, stirring regularly, until lightly browned and aromatic. Each time you finish stirring, level off the flour in the pan so it toasts evenly underneath. It will start to smoke as the flour starts to brown, so stir more regularly so it browns evenly and doesn't become too dark. This process can take 20–25 minutes.

Remove the pan from the heat and put the flour directly into the food processor along with the dates, ground cardamom, fennel and ghee. Pulse it occasionally until all the ingredients are mixed and start to stick together.

To check the consistency of the mixture, scoop out a small spoonful, press the mixture between your fingers to check it will form a truffle. It should stick together easily.

Take 1 tablespoon of the mixture and shape it into a round truffle, pressing it into shape with your hands so it binds together. As you shape the truffles, lay them on the prepared board, baking sheet or cooling rack.

When you've used up all the mixture, take one truffle and dip half of it in the melted chocolate, allowing any excess to drip off the end, then dip into the finely chopped pistachios. Sit the truffle with the chocolate upright on the parchment paper and allow the chocolate to set.

Coat and decorate the rest of the truffles. Once they have set, arrange on a plate and serve.

EID KAAK

These lovely date biscuits look a little like French croissant but are in fact filled with a tantalising combination of spices and soft sweet dates. They're made with a rich buttery pastry, using soured cream to bind, which makes it extra flavoursome. Mahlab is a spice made from a specific cherry stone and has a nutty, slightly bitter taste.

Makes 20

For the dough
60g/½ cup plain flour, sifted, plus extra to dust
60g/½ cup self-raising flour, sifted
40g/⅖ sticks unsalted butter, melted and cooled
75ml/⅓ cup soured cream

For the filling
100g/½ cup pitted, ready-to-eat dates
2 tablespoons boiling water
¼ tsp olive oil, plus extra for greasing
a good pinch of cinnamon, plus extra for dusting

For the spice mix
scant ¼ tsp ground fennel
scant ¼ tsp ground aniseed
scant ¼ tsp ground mahlab

To decorate
icing sugar, for dusting

Preheat the oven to 180°C fan/400°F/gas mark 6. Lightly oil a baking sheet.

Mix all the spices together in a small bowl.

Put both the flours into a large mixing bowl and stir in ½ teaspoon of the spice mixture. Make a well in the centre and add the melted butter and soured cream. Mix together to make a dough. Bring together with your hands and knead very lightly on a clean work surface until smooth. Divide the dough in 2, shape each into a disc, then wrap in clingfilm and chill for 20 minutes.

Make the filling. Put the dates into a food processor with the boiling water. Blitz to make a smooth purée. Add the remaining spice mix, the olive oil and a good pinch of cinnamon and blend again. Tip out onto a plate and divide the date mixture into 20 even-sized balls. Dampen your fingers slightly to help roll if it feels very sticky.

Dust a clean work surface with flour and roll out one piece of dough until it makes a circle of about 20–22cm/8–9in in diameter. Use a plate to cut out a neat circle and a sharp knife to divide it into 10 triangles, like the slices of a pie. Do the same with the other piece of dough.

Take one date paste ball and roll into a thin sausage, the same length as the widest part of the dough triangle.

Take one of the triangles and place the long thin roll of the date paste across the wide base. Roll it up from the wide end, then shape the ends down slightly towards each other to create a little bend so that it looks like a small croissant.

Do the same again with the other pieces of dough to make 20 pieces in total. Transfer to the baking sheet and bake for 10–15 minutes until golden.

Dust with cinnamon and icing sugar before serving.

DATE AND WALNUT NO-CHURN ICE CREAM

This ice cream consists of caramelised walnuts and dates stirred into a whipped sweet condensed milk and double cream base. There's no need to churn it, thanks to the whipping stage – it's frozen in a container and scooped out straight from that. A rich-tasting chocolate sauce completes the feast.

Serves 4–6

sunflower oil, for greasing
100g/½ cup caster sugar
50g/⅜ cup walnuts, chopped
397g/14oz can condensed milk
300ml/1¼ cup double cream
1 tsp vanilla extract
200ml/⅘ cup whipping cream
150g/⅞ cup Medjool dates,
    pitted and chopped

For the chocolate sauce
150g/5oz dark plain chocolate
    (at least 60% cocoa solids),
    finely chopped or grated
5 tbsp whipping cream
1 tbsp golden syrup
a pinch of salt

Lightly oil a metal baking sheet. Spread the sugar in an even layer over the base of a non-stick frying pan. Heat the sugar over a medium heat until it begins to dissolve around the edges. Gently swirl the pan and continue heating until the sugar has completely dissolved and turned into a deep golden caramel.

Remove the pan from the heat and stir in the chopped walnuts, then carefully pour onto the baking sheet. Cool, then break or chop into small pieces.

To make the ice cream, pour the condensed milk, double cream and vanilla extract into a bowl and whisk until very thick and quite stiff. In a separate bowl, whisk the whipping cream until light and fluffy. Gently fold the whipped cream into the condensed milk mixture with the dates and half of the caramelised walnuts. Pour into a 1 litre/1¾ pint freezer container and freeze overnight.

To make the chocolate sauce, put the chocolate and cream into a small pan. Heat gently over a low heat until the chocolate has melted, stirring occasionally. Stir in the golden syrup and salt and serve warm.

To serve, scoop the ice cream into serving dishes, spoon over the warm chocolate sauce and sprinkle with reserved walnuts.

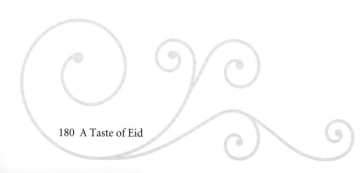

PLANNING A FEAST

A perfect menu is a mixture of flavours, textures and colours and a delight to your guests. With this in mind and whether you're celebrating Eid or getting together for another special occasion, here are a selection of meal plans that gather recipes from this book to inspire your own feasts.

Family Breakfast
Easy Homemade Granola
Balaleet
Khameer Bread
with cream cheese and dates
Apple and Turmeric Booster

Weekend Brunch
Khabeesa
Yogurt with Sweet-and-Sour Chickpeas
Crisp Filo Parcels with Leftover Lamb
Pomegranate and Ginger Sparkler

Lunch
Koftat Samak
Sehnah Tacos
Pistachio, Cranberry and Coconut Burfi
Fresh Lemonade with Mint
Karak Tea or Arabic coffee

Light Lunch (vegetarian)
Grilled Vegetable Kebabs
Rice & Lentil Pilaf
Rangina

Afternoon Tea
Chicken with Mango Chutney and Lime
Dahi Barras
Mini Spiced Date Loaves
Fresh Lemonade with Mint

Dinner (vegetarian)
Selection of appetisers: Tabbouleh,
Moutabel and Hummus with flatbread
Lentil Soup
Vegetable Beryani
Date & Walnut No-Churn Ice Cream
Karak Tea or Arabic coffee

Dinner
Selection of appetisers: Tabbouleh,
Moutabel and Hummus with flatbread
Seafood Soup
Lamb Ghouzi
Lemon-Rose Eid cake
Pomegranate and Ginger Sparkler
Karak Tea or Arabic coffee

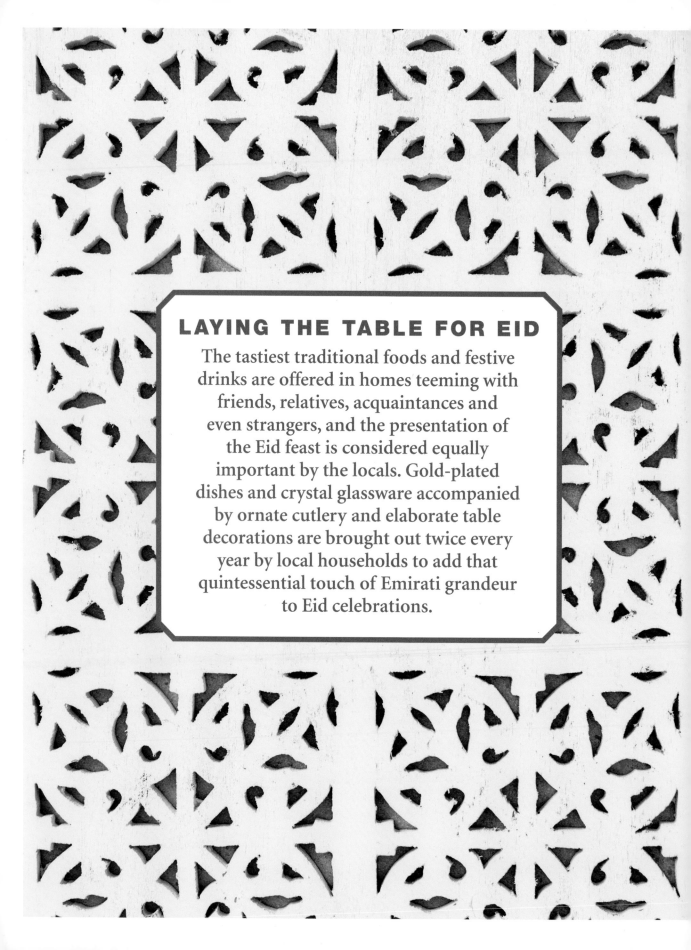

LAYING THE TABLE FOR EID

The tastiest traditional foods and festive drinks are offered in homes teeming with friends, relatives, acquaintances and even strangers, and the presentation of the Eid feast is considered equally important by the locals. Gold-plated dishes and crystal glassware accompanied by ornate cutlery and elaborate table decorations are brought out twice every year by local households to add that quintessential touch of Emirati grandeur to Eid celebrations.

INDEX

INDEX

INDEX

ACKNOWLEDGEMENTS

Thank you to the following chefs, cooks, writers and contributors who have helped in putting this cookbook together.

Reethika Singh (Cupcakeree.com): Easy Homemade Granola; Banana, Mango and Papaya Smoothie

Chef Amna Al Hashemi, co-owner and chef at Mitts & Trays: Balaleet; Chebab with Date Molasses; Khabeesa; Dango; Chammi Dates; Vegetable & Oat Soup; Prawn Biryani; Sago Pudding; Bathitha Truffles; Karak Tea; Mini Spiced Date Loaves; Khabeesa Trifle

Maha Al Mazrouei, owner of the Mellow Yellow Bakeshop and Cafe, Dubai: Barley, Pomegranate and Chamee Salad

Chef Musabbeh Al Kaabi, Executive Oriental Chef at Jumeirah Zabeel Saray, Dubai: Aseeda Bobar; Harees; Hatta Roll with Camel Sour Cream Sauce; Traditional Vegetable Salona

Chef Fatema Showaiter for the Etihad Museum, Emirati Chef in Sharjah: Sehnah Tacos; Muhammar Rice and Fried Safi Fish; Khanfaroosh; Cardamom Scones & Everything Nice

Saliha Mahmood Ahmed: Mutton & Lentil Haleem Stew

Robina Choudhary: Chicken and Chickpea Curry; Chicken Kebabs with Yogurt Dressing

Chef Ali Ebdowa, Mezlai, Emirates Palace, Abu Dhabi: Prawns Irseyah

Sadia Hussain (www.familyfooddiaries.com): Dahi Barras

Khulood Atiq: Khanfaroush (from the cookbook *Sarareed*)

Sheikha Almazrouei: Dates Bethetha

Shaikha Al Ali, Emirati Chef: Halwat Al Tamur Bil Rutab; Ghuraiba Biscuits; Lgeimat; Rangina

Nazrana Saheb (**www.nazzybaker.com**): Pistachio, Cranberry and Coconut Burfi

Walla Abu Eid (@bakemucakeby_walla), mother of three, foodie and baker: Eid Kaak

Kefah Saleh Al Shehhi: Qurs

Afroz Shaikh: Raan Mussallum

Chef Ali Al Neyadi: Margouga Al Dajaj and Lamb Thareed

Sheerin Aswat: cultural researcher

The hand-modelling team: Sheerin Aswat, Amber Choudhary, Bei Guo and Helen Clifford and Yasmin Aswat for her beautiful henna art.

The food writing and testing team: Val Barrett, Jan Fullwood, Anne Harnan, Angela Nilsen and Vicky Musselman

Al Fanar Restaurant & Café, Al Majaz, Sharjah

Al Bait Sharjah, GHM Hotel

Midas PR